MW00526852

DISCARDED
WORTHINGTON LIBRARIES

CHARGING
AHEAD

CHARGING AHEAD

GM, MARY BARRA,
AND THE
REINVENTION
OF AN
AMERICAN ICON

DAVID WELCH

HARPERCOLLINS
LEADERSHIP

AN IMPRINT OF HARPERCOLLINS

© 2022 David Welch

All rights reserved. No portion of this book may be reproduced, stored in a retrieval system, or transmitted in any form or by any means—electronic, mechanical, photocopy, recording, scanning, or other—except for brief quotations in critical reviews or articles, without the prior written permission of the publisher.

Published by HarperCollins Leadership, an imprint of HarperCollins Focus LLC.

Any internet addresses, phone numbers, or company or product information printed in this book are offered as a resource and are not intended in any way to be or to imply an endorsement by HarperCollins Leadership, nor does HarperCollins Leadership vouch for the existence, content, or services of these sites, phone numbers, companies, or products beyond the life of this book.

ISBN 978-1-4002-3360-1 (eBook)
ISBN 978-1-4002-3359-5 (HC)

Library of Congress Control Number: 2022935923

Printed in the United States of America
22 23 24 25 26 LSC 10 9 8 7 6 5 4 3 2 1

CONTENTS

CONTENTS

FOREWORD

On December 10, 2013, at 8:46 a.m., Bloomberg News, in a 1,000-word first draft, informed the world of the biggest business scoop of the year: Mary Barra, whose career began on the factory floor as an intern, would succeed Dan Akerson as chief executive officer of General Motors Co., the first woman CEO in the global automotive industry.

The extent to which Bloomberg owned the story was revealed in the ensuing edition of *Bloomberg Businessweek*, featuring Barra posed with arms crossed in a black-and-white portrait taken the same day, according to an editor's note, and with "The New General" plastered in blue block letters on its cover.

While the world was surprised to learn a fifty-one-year-old woman engineer was the winner over three men (president of GM North America, chief financial officer, and vice chairman), each of whom seemed probable successors to Akerson, Bloomberg was prepared to anoint Barra because its reporters and editors were three years into the twenty-three-year-old news organization's Women Initiative, attempting to narrow gender imbalance in coverage and, especially, its own newsroom. The focus on women protagonists and their voices brought Bloomberg News closer to Barra than it otherwise would have been.

Twelve months earlier, Bloomberg Television anchor Matt Miller was at the 2013 North American International Auto Show in Detroit asking Barra about the Cadillac ATS compact luxury sedan as North American Car of the Year and about the luxury-car market. In March, Barra and Miller discussed GM's products for the Chinese market at the New York International Auto Show. These interviews and several others that followed during the year encouraged our thinking that Barra would emerge as the front-runner to succeed Akerson.

When Akerson showed up at a Bloomberg new office celebration in Southfield on June 17, he did nothing to discourage the possibility that a woman would run GM someday. Thanks to him, Barra was GM's first female chief product officer, the job historically known as the "No. 1 car guy." Akerson had already hinted during a *Wall Street Journal* forum on women executives in 2012 that Barra could advance if GM profitability improved. It had by the time he could chat with us about the layout of our newest newsroom.

By August, *Bloomberg Businessweek*'s David Welch reported in a Bloomberg News "Cars" column that at least four executives were contending to lead GM amid anticipation that Akerson would retire within three years. But Barra and North America president Mark Reuss were the only names mentioned in the piece. A month later, Akerson signaled change was coming.

"The Detroit Three are all run by non-car guys," he said in Detroit. "Someday, there will be a Detroit Three that's run by a car gal."

Barra proved to be fearless and farsighted in ways even Alfred Sloan would admire, not least of all because she questioned everything GM did, including the relevance of the global empire he built. That was revealed for the first time in September 2019 by Welch and Bryan Gruley in the *Bloomberg Businessweek* feature "Mary Barra Bets Big for GM's Electric, Self-Drive Future."

"There was a point in time where we were everywhere for everyone with everything," she told the reporters in an interview at her downtown Detroit office. "We had to say, OK, where are we deploying capital that's not generating appropriate returns? Once you start to believe in the science of global warming and look at the regulatory environment around the world, it becomes pretty clear that to win in the future, you've got to win" with electric and driverless vehicles. "This is what we really believe is the future of transportation."

Here is that story from Bloomberg News Detroit Bureau Chief Welch. He began covering the auto industry for *Business-Week* in 1999, and he proves in this beautifully told tale of redemption for the once great symbol of American manufacturing that luck begins when preparation meets opportunity.

Matthew Winkler
Cofounder and editor-in-chief emeritus
Bloomberg News

CHAPTER 1

⚡

A ROUGH START

It's not even three months into Mary Barra's tenure as chief executive officer of General Motors in April 2014 and already she's having one of the worst weeks of her career. She's in Washington to sit before a congressional panel, where a subcommittee is set to grill the new CEO about a faulty ignition switch that had been linked at that point to thirteen deaths. The infamous switch in GM's Chevrolet Cobalt compact car tended to slip into the "accessory" position while driving, cutting power to the engine and airbags as well as the power breaks and power steering.

The crisis exploded on January 31, just two weeks into her tenure. GM first announced that it needed to recall 778,000 cars because of the bad switch. The number quickly grew to 1.6 million, then 2.6 million. Early on, GM North America president Alan Batey publicly apologized, and the company advised its customers that the switch could turn off while in the drive position if the key is on a key ring that was laden with heavy items. The explanation also came off as flimsy, almost blaming car owners who might have had a monstrosity of trinkets and keys on their keychains. As ridiculous as these keychains look, with rabbit's feet, fuzzy dice, and other tchotchkes attached to clattering rings of keys, people do that all the time.

More details came to light courtesy of plaintiffs' attorneys who were suing the company. The narrative that was unfolding would soon de-pants GM. Lawsuits revealed that company engineers and attorneys knew the switch was problematic for more than a decade and never issued a recall. One manager nixed a remedy saying it was too expensive. That larded-up cost? Fifty-seven cents per car, about the price of greasy diner coffee. True to GM's notorious culture of ignoring problems and shirking accountability, nothing was done. Some engineers even covered it up to save face internally. The Justice Department opened a probe, Congress wanted answers, and Barra had to take the heat. As if anything could be more embarrassing for a company that had survived its 2009 bankruptcy only with the last-chance lifeline of government money, it was about to be humiliated again.

That bailout hung over the proceedings. President Barack Obama's Auto Task Force had played a key role in restructuring the company in 2009 and helped create a new GM with a solid balance sheet, more focused family of brands, and a profitable business. It was clear, however, that while the government was funding GM, some insiders were either hiding the deadly ignition problem or, at best, not doing their duty to protect customers.

At the time that the switch was being put into GM's compact Chevy cars at a factory in Ohio, Barra had been managing a Cadillac plant in Detroit. Her career path kept her well away from the troubled car until January. But there she was in Washington on April 1. Barra and GM's management team still didn't have an explanation for how the bad switch got through the company's engineering process, why it wasn't

fixed when problems surfaced, and who knew what and when.
She had hired an outside law firm to investigate the whole
matter, but had no concrete conclusions yet.

The vaudevillian stage of a congressional hearing is no
place for a rookie CEO. Actually, it's no place for anyone who
doesn't relish the skullduggery of American politics. In 1947,
Howard Hughes managed to turn the tables on a senator from
Maine named Ralph Brewster. But Hughes had the comfort of
his own extreme wealth and the benefit that his accuser was
in the back pocket of his competitor, Pan Am. Since Hughes
took his *bête noire* to the mats, few CEOs have managed to
escape these hearings with anything but a tarring.

Barra had everything working against her. She hadn't had
much time on the public stage and rarely appeared comfortable in the limelight. Details about the switch and what GM
knew were still knotted up in a boondoggle of internal probes,
engineering analyses, and corporate silos that did a poor job of
talking to one another. The engineer responsible for the switch
also made the problem tough to find internally. Pennsylvania
Republican Tim Murphy and Colorado Democrat Diana DeGette
wanted to know why GM had taken so long to find the problem
and recall a switch that was so cheap to fix. They also demanded
to know who in the upper reaches of GM's executive suite knew
about the bad part and when. The Senate hearing the next day
went no better. Claire McCaskill of Missouri and California's
Barbara Boxer laid into Barra over GM's culture of cover-up and
her own inability to provide answers. In both hearings, Barra
deflected questions, blamed pre-bankruptcy GM, and could
mostly say that the company was investigating the matter.

"I cannot tell you why it took so long for a safety defect to
be announced for this program, but I can tell you we will find
out," Barra said, adding later that, "all I can tell you is that at
today's GM, we are focused on safety."

The hearing came off so badly that it was parodied four days later as the cold open sketch on *Saturday Night Live*. Kate McKinnon delivers a hilarious performance as a clueless, dodging Mary Barra. The video clip was shared all over social media, reaching the entire auto industry and her peers at the highest levels of the Fortune 500. It was a hard sketch, too. When asked why GM didn't make the recall years earlier, McKinnon's Barra said, "We're looking into that. I can't speak to how the old GM would handle that. I can only speak to the new GM." When the parody version of Murphy asked when Barra knew about the defect, McKinnon said, "I am looking into knowing when I first knew about it, but I won't know about the results of that knowing until I know for sure."

Her week in Washington had the opposite impact of the famous 1952 hearing where GM president Charlie Wilson charmed the Senate after being nominated as secretary of defense under President Dwight Eisenhower. Wilson famously said that "for years I thought that what was good for our country was good for General Motors, and vice versa. The difference did not exist. Our company is too big. It goes with the welfare of the country. Our contribution to the nation is considerable."

To American viewers, it was the other way around. The nation's contribution to GM was more than it got back. The US Treasury put more than $50 billion into GM in 2009 and got about $40 billion back out. Saving GM and Chrysler—and by extension preserving the parts companies that supply Ford, Toyota, Honda, and the rest—for a net payout of $11 billion is an absolute bargain. Without question, the Obama administration saved the US auto industry. But that doesn't gloss over the fact that while the Treasury Department was funding GM and helping to restructure the company, unsafe cars were on the road. And it certainly underscored GM's reputation for failure. The undercurrent of the hearings could be summed up with a rhetorical question: "This is what we saved?"

It wasn't supposed to go this way. Barra was named as the CEO of GM in December 2013 and became a sensation almost overnight. It was a coming-of-age moment for her and for women in business. America had seen female CEOs at iconic companies. There is Indra Nooyi at Pepsi, Meg Whitman with Hewlett-Packard, and Marillyn Hewson at Lockheed Martin, to name a few. But this was a car company, and not just any automaker. It was GM. The General. America's once iconic industrial giant was back in business.

GM had suffered years of decline before going bankrupt, but it really isn't just any other company. It once was the world's most dominant carmaker. Its factories helped build the arsenal of democracy that freed Europe from Nazi Germany and defeated the fascist Empire of Japan. Chevys and Cadillacs are woven into American culture and sung about by artists from Don McLean to Bruce Springsteen to Snoop Dogg. The company's economic might, as Charlie Wilson pointed out, provided a livelihood for millions of people for more than a century. America without GM is like America without the Yankees.

Under CEO Dan Akerson, who was instrumental in Barra's rise to the top, the company had a newfound sense of stability. Right before Barra took the job, the US Treasury had sold the last of its GM stock that it got as part of the bailout. It was "Government Motors" no more. Akerson had put out some of the fires. It was up to Barra to remake the company.

She had a vision for it, too. Barra's father was a United Auto Workers factory hand in Pontiac in the days when every other car bought in America was made by GM. Her vision was restoring the company to a leadership position, one that made great cars and also led the way with new technology as it did in its heyday of the 1960s. The company had prototypes of electric cars well before Tesla's Elon Musk was even born. GM engineers had toyed with the idea of embedding wires in the roads that would use radio signals to help cars drive themselves. No, Google did not dream up the autonomous car. GM also pioneered the EV1 electric car in the 1990s, making it the first modern-era EV before fumbling away that early advantage.

Barra's vision wasn't fully formed and she hadn't articulated it externally, but she could see that the world was getting closer to the biggest change to transportation since gasoline engines replaced steam and horses. Tesla had proven that luxury buyers like electric cars. In China, where GM is a top player, Barra saw the government ushering in an era of electrification with strong incentives and mandates. Across the globe, climate change was becoming a more pressing issue all the time. With emissions rules getting tougher, cars that ran on fossil fuels were getting more expensive to make thanks to all of that clean-air hardware they needed. She wanted to lead that generational change rather than let Tesla own it.

When she was officially named to the job, media reports were glowing. If a woman could take the top job at a stodgy old company like GM and break through the macho edifice of the male-dominated car business, then women could truly lead anywhere. And she was an engineer, not a finance guy like the executives who ran the company during its decline. Effusive headlines poured off the web.

- "At last, Detroit has some girl power," crowed *Forbes*.[1]
- General Motors is "smashing a century-old gender barrier," wrote the *Wall Street Journal*.[2]
- Longtime industry analyst Michelle Krebs summed it up more bluntly for the *Guardian*: "My first comment

to colleagues was: 'Holy shit!' I honestly didn't think this would happen in my lifetime."[3]

- *New York Times* writer Bill Vlasic wrote that Barra had "gasoline running through her veins."

Ever the team player, when Barra addressed GM's workforce at a town hall meeting in Detroit, the message wasn't about her or about breaking the glass ceiling. It was about taking the once-iconic automaker from its fall from grace to a new era of respectability and then on to greatness. That's the same vision that she described to Ed Whitacre, the retired AT&T chairman, five years earlier in 2009 when he was CEO after the company's bankruptcy.

"This is truly the next chapter in GM's recovery and turnaround history," Barra told employees when she got the job. "And I'm proud to be a part of it."

If Barra were the type for self-congratulation (she most certainly is not), it would have been a short celebration. How she faced the ignition crisis would be make-or-break for GM's reputation and its future. Even without the crisis, she had a list of problems that had to be fixed before she could start to push for the kind of GM that she envisioned. Aside from the US and China, most of GM's other operations lost money. Barra's GM couldn't think like old GM where being the biggest in the world mattered.

GM operated in more than 100 countries and spent a fortune developing and marketing cars across the globe. Most of the global business just siphoned cash from the company. The European business, anchored by Germany's Opel brand, which legendary company president Alfred Sloan acquired in 1929, lost on average $1 billion a year.

"The company was still in deep trouble," said Tim Solso, who was on GM's board and named non-executive chairman when Barra was named CEO. "It was unacceptable. All of the international operations had low market share and were losing money. There was still a culture that said we had to be the biggest."

That culture needed a reboot. Barra may have deflected a lot of questions in Washington that week in April, but in her testimony was an important answer that was at the heart of her vision for the company. Murphy had asked her if GM's excessive focus on cost led the company to make the ill-fated decision on the ignition switch. Barra didn't argue the point. GM's retiree costs had grown out of control. In 2003, when GM engineers were preparing to build the Cobalt, the company issued $17.6 billion in debt to raise money for its pension funds because it wasn't generating enough cash to pay its bills. Medical costs rose every year for its legions of U.S. retirees. The net result: the automaker carried a $1,600 per vehicle burden for retirees that rivals like Toyota and Honda didn't have. GM was constantly cutting corners on its vehicles. Every penny was counted. Bankruptcy wiped away much of that burden, but Barra still needed to get a company that counted pennies and paper clips to think more about customers.

"That's not how we do business in today's GM," she told Murphy. "In general we've moved from a cost culture after the bankruptcy to a customer culture."

Her answer probably sounded like pabulum to members of Congress, but it was at the core of what she hoped to do with GM. If she could get through the crisis with her career and GM's reputation intact, she knew exactly what she wanted to do. She and Mark Reuss, another GM lifer who had Barra's old job running product development, had decided that there would be "no more crappy cars." Dan Ammann had been promoted from chief finance officer to company president and put in place a system to track how much money GM was making or losing on every car in every market around the globe. GM managers could no longer hide underperforming cars or businesses. Barra wanted to root out the excuse making and tolerance for losing that had been part of GM's culture. In 2015, she told me that she had had enough of the "dog ate my homework" excuses.[4]

The new developments in technology that shaped Barra's vision for GM were also threats to the company. The day before she took over as CEO, Tesla had announced that its Model S sedan had sold 22,300 vehicles in 2013. That's a pittance for a GM that sold 9 million cars a year, but that Model S typically went out the door for more than $100,000 and was stealing luxury buyers at the expense of Cadillac and the likes of BMW, Lexus, and Mercedes. Even at those prices, the Model S was close to outselling the Nissan Leaf EV and GM's Chevy Volt, which ran on gasoline and a battery. Many people in Detroit were dismissive of Elon Musk, but he was about to turn transportation as we know it on its head. And he could fund it, too. No matter how much money Tesla lost, investors just gave him more.

While Musk was forging a lead in electric drive, Google's self-driving car project was already testing a two-seat, egg-shaped pod that could drive itself. It wasn't fast and certainly not ready to take on America's highways, but it was progress. Meanwhile, Uber Technologies was in the process of doubling ridership compared to the year before and becoming a phenomenon. Both had the ability to fundamentally change how people get around.

Barra would need billions to compete with Silicon Valley's push into transportation. She didn't have Tesla's seemingly bottomless well of cash from Wall Street. Nor did she have Google's $65 billion war chest. She wasn't going to get it by losing money the world over as the old GM did. She would

CHARGING AHEAD

also have to hire the kind of talent and knowhow to engineer the future of transport. As tough as it is for those companies to start new businesses, Barra's task ahead was also a difficult one. She had to retool a 110-year-old company that had forgotten how to win. She would need to be ruthless and decisive, and also imaginative.

10

CHAPTER 2

THE FAMILY BUSINESS

Mary Teresa Makela, the woman who would eventually set out to remake GM, was born on Christmas Eve, 1961, just a week away from what would kick off one of the best years in the company's history. During the first year of her life, GM would own almost 52 percent of the US car market. The company brought in huge profits and presided over a dominant global empire. It had such a lead on Ford, Chrysler, and American Motors in the US that Alfred Sloan, the company's legendary chairman who at that point sat on the board in an honorary position, feared the Justice Department would break it up.

The economy was growing robustly in the early 1960s and Americans were developing a growing love affair with cars and the freedom they could bring. Expanding suburbs meant Americans wanted more wheels and GM was in the pole position to provide them. Sales rose 30 percent in 1962 in the US and revenue rose almost as fast to $14.6 billion. The bottom line got even fatter. Profits rose 63 percent to $1.5 billion. That's $14 billion in 2022 dollars in net income, which is more than Barra's GM has ever made in a year—and her GM makes good money. Even though market share fell in 1963, profits grew yet again. GM was the most profitable company in the world, according to the *New York Times.*

When Barra was growing into her toddler years, Cadillac was the unquestioned luxury leader. Its 1957 Eldorado Brougham sold for more than $13,000, not far off the price of a Rolls-Royce Silver Cloud. The Chevrolet Impala sedan was America's favorite car. In 1965 alone, Chevy sold 1.1 million Impalas in a car market that bought up about 8 million vehicles. One in seven cars sold was an Impala. I would later learn to drive in my father's blue, 1985 Impala wagon. It was America's family car for decades.

The GM that Barra grew up with was the Yankees in the DiMaggio years. It was the biggest and richest company in the world. Sloan's loose governance structure, in which the Cadillac, Buick, Oldsmobile, Pontiac, GMC, and Chevrolet divisions operated independently but with Sloan's own central control of the finances, had been profiled in management guru Peter Drucker's book *Concept of the Corporation.* Decades earlier, Donaldson Brown had brought chemical giant DuPont's accounting methods to GM and improved them, revolutionizing how companies tracked money. The company's success was one of the shiniest emblems of American's post-war ascension.

GM was viewed as the paragon of business management and the most respected company in the world. Its might and importance at the time cannot be overstated. In the 1920s, GM invented automotive styling under the leadership of legendary designer Harley Earl. He developed the first full-scale design studio, called the "Art and Color Section," and retired in 1958, leaving GM as a styling leader. His last designs were in showrooms when Barra was born. His crew invented tail fins, which were a fashion mainstay throughout the 1960s.

During World War II, GM plants made M-4 "Sherman" and M-5 tanks, B-24 bombers, and millions of ammunition casings. They churned out Hellcat antitank guns and armored cars. Detroit's industrial might (which included Ford and a handful of other smaller carmakers) was a symbol of national pride, seen as the power and muscle that won the war and made America the eminent global power in the years after.

GM was the biggest of them and at the time, the smartest. Its R&D group made a pump that was used in the first open-heart surgery. GM and Boeing engineered the Apollo 15 lunar rover. The company made the first diesel-electric locomotive, replacing the sooty steam engines that clanked across the American West. Its Frigidaire appliance division made refrigerators a household commodity. In the 1980s, Mercedes cars came into the US without air conditioning. They installed GM's ACDelco air because it was the best in the industry.

Today, some Americans see GM as just another company selling pickup trucks and SUVs. Many others view the company as a symbol of America's industrial decline. Its share of the US market is around 17 percent. The profits are strong, but it is far smaller.

During the company's heyday, GM was a wealth-generating machine. In 1962, GM's annual report showed that the company paid its investors $863 million. That's $7.8 billion in dividends in 2021 dollars, almost four times what the company pays today. GM paid out $111 million in pensions that year, or $1 billion today. The automaker employed 605,000 workers, more than the population of Milwaukee. That year alone, GM's payroll was almost $4 billion. That translates to $36 billion today. More than half were hourly factory workers who made an average of $136 a week. Adjusted for inflation, that pay equals about $29 an hour, which is close to the top UAW wage today. Back then it was a real middle-class wage. The average family made $6,000 a year, according to the US Census Department. GM's union factory hands earned more than $7,000.

GM created a way of life for millions of people working not just in its plants, but as parts makers or in railroads, dealerships, and steel mills. One of them was Ray Makela, Barra's father. He was a die maker in GM's Pontiac Motor Works, where the company had a massive manufacturing complex. In the parlance of union culture, Makela was a skilled tradesman. Tool and die workers made the heavy equipment that produced car body panels, fenders, and other of the 30,000 parts needed to build a car.

Barra's mother, Eva, née Pyykkonen, was a bookkeeper and seamstress. Neither had gone to college but they were insistent that Mary and her brother, Paul, get an education.[1] Both parents were of Finnish descent and Barra herself will occasionally talk with pride about being Scandinavian. On their income, the Makelas could afford to live in Waterford, a mostly white, middle-class community dotted with small lakes north of Pontiac. Back then, when Barra went to Waterford Mott High School, the whole area was solidly middle class and still is. Ray Makela had secure work at GM's 120-acre industrial complex in Pontiac.

So did thousands of others. Pontiac had four assembly plants as well as a stamping operation that pressed out body panels. The Pontiac Truck & Coach division, which made trucks and buses, was based there. The Pontiac Car division built storied names like the Bonneville sedan, Grand Prix coupe, and Tempest Le Mans convertible. Eventually, the plant made the legendary GTO muscle car.

As a student at Waterford Mott, Barra was conscientious. Her favorite subject was math, which inspired her to major in electrical engineering in college. That was a rare choice for women in the 1980s. Her parents encouraged her to pursue it. She also graduated at the top of her class with a 4.0 GPA and was named "Most Likely to Succeed."[2]

When Barra graduated in 1979, GM was still easily the world's biggest carmaker. Its share of the US market had declined but was still a staggering 45 percent. Margins were falling, too, but being big and still very profitable gave its top brass plenty of reason to be complacent. In its annual report to shareholders, the company bragged that sales were their third best ever and the year saw its fourth best profits.

There were signs that GM's decades of dominance were under threat. In his letter to stockholders that year, Chairman Tom Murphy bemoaned that rising fuel prices and gasoline shortages had pushed Americans to swiftly change how they bought vehicles. They were passing up on trucks and big cars and opting for small, fuel-efficient models. Compact cars were never Detroit's forte and the profits were meager compared to big sedans and pickups.

Mary Barra might not have known that GM was starting to lose its grip, either. She was preparing to leave Waterford Mott for Michigan State and wondering how she would pay for it. Her parents had enough saved only for her freshman year. When a friend told her about General Motors Institute's Co-Op program, in which she could work for the automaker to help pay for school, she applied. With her grades and aptitude, she was a cinch to get in.[3]

She started in 1980, majoring in electrical engineering, when at most 15 percent of the students were women, said Mo Torfeh, an Iranian-born engineering professor at General Motors Institute (GMI), now called Kettering University. He said Barra was one of his favorite students. The fact that there were few women didn't faze her, he said. Studying engineering at a mostly male college that fed students to a male-dominated company like GM set Barra on a path to navigate the minority status of being a woman for the rest of her career.

Torfeh said his female students worked harder because they felt they had something to prove. Barra was no exception. She sat at the front of the class and studied hard. She never made an issue of being a woman. Quite the opposite, he said. She was smart, friendly, and a consensus builder in her group lab work. She was respected by her classmates for being an organizer and taskmaster, while taking charge in a collegial way. She would assign the work and check in on her team members, said Torfeh. The group had to develop a controller for a battery-powered electric motor. It had to put out 300 rpm, Torfeh said, not 280 or 310. It had to be exact and stable.

"She made sure that the other teammates did their part," he said. "You could see that she wanted to be leading. She liked to take charge, but she was respectful. They did well on the project and she got an A in the class."

Her first job as a GM co-op student was at the Fiero plant in Pontiac, not far from where her father had worked before retiring a few years earlier. Upon her graduation in 1985, she went to work as a facilities engineer and supervisor at a time when GM was trying to pioneer a new production system based on Toyota's lean manufacturing methods. Her job was to supervise skilled tradesmen and make sure everything kept running smoothly.

Tim Lee, who later retired from GM as head of manufacturing, was assigned as plant manager at Fiero in 1987. At thirty-seven, he was the youngest plant manager the company ever had. His first move was to look at the power distribution system in the plant. If that goes down, production comes to a halt immediately.

"You want to know all the shit that can go wrong," Lee said. "I asked for the plant floor electrical foreman to take me on a tour. Meet me at column A 12. Here walks up this petite woman, radio strapped to her waist and tools hanging off her belt."

That image sums up Barra in many ways. She's small in stature but effective at what she does. She always went about her assignments in sleeves-up fashion. "She wasn't flashy," Lee said.

At the time, GM had a joint venture in Fremont, California, with Toyota New United Motor Manufacturing, Inc., or NUMMI. GM was trying to learn from the Japanese carmaker why its plants were so efficient and produced such quality cars. One of Toyota's innovations was enabling line workers to stop production when they saw a problem, which gave people on the plant floor a big voice in running production. They could pull a line called the Andon Cord, which would set off a chime and stop the line. Then engineers and other workers would rush to the scene to see what happened.

The chime went off from the paint shop one day, said Cheri Alexander, who was a manager in the plant and now is a business professor at University of Michigan. In auto plants, paint shops are vital, and stoppages are costly. You need to keep the paint flowing through the tubes and sprayers or it can get gummed up. When Alexander arrived on the third floor, Barra was already on the scene, holding court with eight engineers and paint-shop workers.

"We hurried up there," Alexander said. "When I got there, there was Mary with about eight of her workers. She was listening intently. She went around and listened to all of these men. They were all bigger, taller, and older. She was probably twenty-six. Her team found a solution and got the line moving again in eighteen minutes. That was the moment I knew we had something special," Alexander said.

Lee liked her, too. He promoted her to supervisor during her two-year stint at the plant. By many measures, the factory was a success. It had strong productivity and was one of GM's best plants in terms of quality, Alexander said. But in what would become a recurring theme during Barra's ascent at GM, her best efforts and the work of her team would end up being futile because of greater forces around them. The Fiero plant was ultimately doomed due to the car itself being so flawed.

The little Fiero was designed as a sporty competitor to Japanese two-seaters like the Toyota MR2 and Mazda RX-7. Pontiac hoped it would bring back young buyers who liked sporty cars, but the Fiero was junk. Engineered for fuel economy, it didn't have the zip of those cars. The MR2 had 122 horsepower and the Fiero's "Iron Duke" four-cylinder engine kicked with only ninety-two horses. Instead of a hip new Pontiac, it was yet another symbol of Japanese superiority. *Car and Driver* writer Rich Ceppos recalled how disappointing the car was. "Back then we were so bereft of good domestic cars it seemed like a ray of hope," he wrote. "Everyone hoped it would be something else. But it was crap."[4]

Worse, it tended to catch on fire. The car's rear-mounted engine had a small oil pan. When the car ran low on oil, connecting rods could rip through the side of the engine, spraying hot oil on the exhaust manifold, often resulting in a fire. One in 400 Fieros built in 1987 caught on fire and GM had to recall 125,000 of them.[5]

The fires were the last straw. It was an expensive headache for the company and a death knell for the Fiero name. Lee said he arrived in 1987 and found himself closing the plant the next year with the last of the cars rolling off the line in August of 1988.

Such issues were epidemic in the 1980s. GM, Ford, and Chrysler had persistent quality problems that began in the 1970s when Detroit's automakers had to shift from rear-drive cars with big engines to front-drive cars with smaller motors. They couldn't do it fast enough without quality issues.

GM developed other problems in the 1980s under the disastrous reign of Chairman Roger Smith and the years immediately following it. The company had ripped up much of Alfred Sloan's management structure that gave autonomy to each division. In its place, Smith turned a mash-up of divisions into two units, Chevy-Pontiac-Canada (CPC) to make small cars and Buick-Olds-Cadillac (BOC) for large cars. GM divisions lost their autonomy. The cars made by Chevy, Pontiac, Oldsmobile, and Buick shared so many parts that they began to look alike. Some of the Cadillacs did, too. Rick Wagoner, who was CEO from 2000 to 2009, said the new divisional structure just threw GM's experts hither and yon throughout the company, which led to all kinds of problems. GM couldn't get new vehicles out in time and quality suffered.

Rather than focus on the company's look-alike designs and reliability issues, Roger Smith's GM was always looking for a silver bullet solution. He spent $35 billion on robots in GM's plants in an effort to save on labor. But they made quality even worse. In one plant, robots in the paint shop infamously painted each other rather than the cars, the *Wall Street Journal* reported.[6]

He also acquired Ross Perot's Electronic Data Systems to modernize the automaker's processes and systems. That cost $2.5 billion. Perot became a major shareholder and started a series of very public and open boardroom battles. The wily Texan frequently criticized Smith and the board for not fixing their reliability problems or improving styling. The automaker's board later paid Perot more than $700 million to go away.

In 1985, Smith bought Hughes Aircraft for $5.2 billion to diversify into aerospace. He also wanted to take advantage of its electronics and satellite capabilities to modernize the automobile. The latter motive wasn't wrongheaded. Cars would later add more computer capability on board and connect via satellite for safety and communications. GM's OnStar telematics unit was a direct outgrowth of Smith's acquisitions, but his deal making bore little fruit otherwise and he diverted billions from the car business. At the time of the Hughes deal, company critic Ralph Nader said that Smith "should have invested this money into improving its automobile, in fuel efficiency, in quality control, in all the ways they're deficient to the Japanese."[7] He also spent as much as $5 billion creating the Saturn division, with its plastic-bodied compact car, new plant in Tennessee, and unique labor contract.[8] Despite initial success, Saturn eventually hit the shoals due to a lack of new product. GM couldn't afford enough new models for the division. He also tragically underfunded the pension plan.

By 1987, when Barra was wearing a tool belt and troubleshooting the paint shop, market share hit 35 percent. The company was in the midst of closing sixteen plants and cutting 36,000 workers to deal with its falling market share. Smith said they were downsizing to get rid of old, outdated factories.[9] That was partly true, but in reality, he was racing to downsize the company to its true market share. That reality would plague Smith and every CEO who followed him, including Barra.

With the Fiero plant closing down, Barra was out of a job. She would have been able to find another assignment within GM. That wasn't the issue for a manager who was groomed at GMI. Plus, Lee thought she was a real talent, so she would have opportunity. The quandary was more about what she wanted to do next. She decided to apply for a Sloan Fellowship within GM, which would send her to Stanford University or MIT to get an MBA. Barra chose Stanford, where she became the star of the class, said Charles Holloway, now a professor emeritus at Stanford who taught her at the time.

Her experience managing at a plant and working in a giant corporate bureaucracy gave her a perspective that other students didn't have. She also had a gravitas about her, Holloway said. Barra was vocal in class, but her ability to listen and involve others in a discussion made her both authoritative and likable.

"She came in with a lot of background in manufacturing and understanding how big companies ran, but she was very smart and able to articulate her knowledge," Holloway said in an interview. "In class, when there was a discussion, whenever Mary would speak, everyone paid attention."

By the time she graduated from Stanford in 1990, GM was entering a full-blown crisis. Now under Smith's successor, Robert Stempel, the company reported a record loss of $4.5 billion in 1991. Since Smith had blown so much of GM's cash on deals and failed modernization efforts, the company was scraping to fund development of new models that it needed to remain competitive. The company had to go to Wall Street to raise $6 billion, which was a stunning turnabout for a GM that had historically printed money.

Lead director John Smale, a former Procter & Gamble CEO, and outside attorney Ira Millstein worked with GM General Counsel Harry Pearce to get Stempel to resign. They also forced out company president Lloyd Reuss, whose son Mark would later become president under Barra. Stempel had announced a plan to cut 74,000 jobs by 1995. As staggering as that number was, GM wasn't downsizing fast enough. He was fired and the board put Jack Smith in place after a successful run at GM's European Opel business.[10]

Barra survived the company's wrenching overhaul. Her big break came in 1997 when CEO Jack Smith went looking for talented young executives who would shadow him and the top four managers in the company. These were up-and-comers who they thought would benefit from being exposed to every aspect of the business with a view from the C-suite. They would do a two-year stint as executive assistants. Pearce, who had risen to vice chairman after helping to broker Stempel's exit years earlier, asked for names from different managers and Barra's came up. Lee had floated the idea himself and it rose up to Pearce's desk.

He interviewed Barra and was instantly impressed. She didn't have a big ego like many rising managers in the company. She was interested in GM's EV1, the auto industry's first electric car sold to the public in modern times. She also had open eyes when it came to GM's stubborn cultural resistance to new ideas and change.

"From the moment I interviewed her I thought, *wow, she could run the company one day,*" Pearce said. "I realize that's a leap. She wasn't even a plant manager. I thought it was remarkable what her insights were. Even back then she had ideas on how to transform the vehicle."

Since Pearce oversaw GM's investment in new technology, like gasoline-electric hybrids, hydrogen fuel cells, and battery-powered vehicles, he had the EV1 in his domain. They talked about how automobiles had an emissions problem that had made the industry a lightning rod for regulators and environmentalists. The industry had been working on better catalytic converters, which reduce smog-causing emissions, and smaller engines that created less carbon dioxide. But none of that would eliminate emissions as a problem, Pearce said.

GM saw the EV1 as a test bed. The lead-acid battery car was leased in tiny numbers in California and Arizona. But it was an important first step in electrification. Barra agreed and thought GM should try to press ahead with electric technology, Pearce said.

"She was an electrical engineer and saw the potential," Pearce told me. "She just felt that we needed to challenge ourselves in terms of the future of the industry beyond making another car with a few different gadgets. She thought it could be transformative, but she readily admitted that there were all kinds of hurdles. She demonstrated to me a genuine interest in making an effort beyond just R&D."

The EV1 lasted just three years. The program was closed down in 2000 with GM having spent $1 billion on the car, Wagoner said. The company made the car from scratch, he told me, which made it expensive. "We spent so much money on it that it wasn't sustainable. GM had a big advantage and a really good position, but unfortunately way too early," he said. Still, it left an impression with Barra that GM could get ahead of rivals with innovation.

Pearce and Barra also discussed GM's complacent culture. The bad habits from the Roger Smith era had not gone away even though some people in the company were starting to face the fact that GM had lost its way.

"It seemed we were stuck in an ever-repetitive cycle," Pearce said. "Mary and I knew that we had serious quality problems. Jack [Smith] was concerned. Even though we understood how the Japanese worked at quality, the company was so resistant of finding new ways to solve quality problems. Mary's attitude was, you've never got it completely fixed."

The two of them talked about it on a regular basis, Pearce said. GM had denied there were quality issues all the way back to the days of Roger Smith. It set up a culture of shirking accountability. Even into the 2000s, if GM fared poorly in Consumer Reports or J.D. Power quality studies, the company had a habit of saying that the survey was unfair rather than focusing on the problems. Pearce said Barra knew that the company needed to change. The two of them discussed the

THE FAMILY BUSINESS

many bad practices up and down the ladder of management. Good ideas had trouble getting to the top, especially from the company's many factories, where input from lower-level employees was frequently ignored or never even sought out. There was a culture of intimidation left over from the Roger Smith years.

Pearce decided to address it directly to GM's top 3,000 executives at the company's annual retreat in Florida in September 2000. He had Barra prepare a presentation based on their discussions about the company's management and cultural problems. They sent out email surveys and conducted in-person interviews across the globe. In all, Pearce and Barra got 152,000 responses. The presentation had voice-over clips from employees. They didn't pull punches.

"Open, loud, public counseling of subordinates is not acceptable conduct for true leaders," said one employee. "Neither are temper tantrums, use of excessive profanity in business meetings involving direct reports and subordinates, or the walking out of business meetings when the content does not meet expectations."

"There are examples of leaders at all levels in GM that are known for their poor behavior to subordinates," said another. "This type of behavior creates or adds to the culture of fear."

Barra and Pearce took what everyone knew was wrong with GM and served it up cold, in the light of day, to get the problem out there.

"Civility isn't found in these managers' vocabulary as they cling to an old autocratic style," Pearce said in the speech. "This is particularly worrisome because just a few of these people can set the wrong example for hundreds of aspiring leaders who believe this is the path to the top. In our new leadership culture, that behavior needs to be a ticket out— not up."

Office politics were also exposed. GM was notorious as a sharp-elbowed place where managers would try to get to the next level, whatever it took. Longtime Cadillac dealer Martin "Hoot" McInerney once told me that the problem at GM is that most of its executives did their job with one eye on the task at hand and the other on the next promotion.

"The primary problem with leadership is an excessive concern with getting ahead on the corporate ladder," said another employee in the video. "People spend more time on politics than on doing a good job."

Pearce's presentation was pretty damning, but it got a standing ovation, he said. Barra and another of Pearce's assistants wrote it with an upbeat conclusion saying that the company had the right people to change direction. "Now, it's our turn as GM leaders," Pearce said. "We have the people! We have the resources! We have the ideas! Together let's build and nurture the culture that will supercharge this great enterprise into the twenty-first century and beyond."

By the time the presentation was given, Barra had been promoted from Pearce's assistant to director of internal communications. It was the kind of soft management job that big car companies often give to women. They get sent to areas like human resources, marketing, and communications while men get promoted into the more macho, nuts-and-bolts jobs like engineering and manufacturing.

Barra herself was confused by the assignment, she told author Laura Colby.[11] "I was like, I'm an engineer," she said.

Gary Cowger, who was head of manufacturing at the time, gave her the position because she knew her way around plants and could talk to union workers, he told me. More to the point, GM needed a soft touch after a bruising fifty-four-day strike at two plants in Flint that made parts for the rest of GM's other factories. That strike was a low point for GM's relations with its union workers. The company had been closing plants and cutting jobs throughout the '80s and '90s. To lower costs, the company had also been outsourcing to lower-wage suppliers some work that had traditionally been done in its own factories. "Outsourcing" became a dirty word among UAW rank and file.

The union, under fiery president Stephen Yokich, had waged the strike under the pretense of "health and safety issues" and some local production disputes, which was the only legal way it could be done in the middle of an existing labor contract. Since the union had previously agreed to the pay, wages, and jobs, it couldn't legally strike about those issues during the life of the agreement. Yokich knew what he was doing. The two Flint plants were vital for GM. One made metal stampings and the other made multiple parts. If they go down, so would most of GM's North American operations because the assembly plants would run out of essential parts. It's what the union called "a bottleneck strike."

The union was using other justification to send GM a message about job cuts and outsourcing. GM saw the strike as illegal and even sued the union in court over the reasons for the strike. In short, GM said the UAW had ginned up local grievances to start a strike over company-wide issues.

During the strike, I was covering the UAW's Constitutional Congress in Las Vegas as a reporter for the *Fort Worth Star-Telegram*. At the end of each day's business, Yokich would brief the media on the state of the strike. I approached him on the stage to ask a few follow-up questions. When I introduced myself, he asked, "You're from where?"

"Fort Worth," I said.

"Texas?" he said. "You write about labor in Texas? You got balls, kid."

Then he went on a rant about GM and its job cuts. The union could always get things done with Ford and Chrysler, he said. "But with GM there's always a goddamn problem."

In the end, the two Flint plants agreed to boost their productivity by 15 percent. GM dropped its lawsuit. The big conflict over job cuts and outsourcing wasn't resolved. GM would keep cutting jobs well after the strike. The company had no choice, and the union had no leverage to stop it. Lots of bad blood remained.

Part of Barra's new job was to tell an angry workforce at GM's plants that they needed to improve quality and productivity. She set up a system to show workers where they stood against other plants on a variety of metrics. She also had to show workers that GM had more production capacity than the company needed. Cowger had her put a team together to show the union what he called "Business 101" kind of data so they understood why the company was making changes.

"We improved getting knowledge on the floor," Cowger said. "We had way too much capacity for all the market share we had lost. It was a matter of rightsizing infrastructure and capacity. We have to get this place fixed. We took out 3 million units of production with no strikes."

Cowger gave Barra one of her big breaks in 2003 when he asked her to run GM's D-Ham plant, so called because it straddled the line between Detroit and the enclave city of Hamtramck. It was also called Poletown because of Hamtramck's Polish heritage. GM built the plant in 1985 by working with legendary and controversial Detroit mayor Coleman Young. Mayor Young used eminent domain to relocate 1,400 houses and their families along with several churches. The local community was outraged; some people had to be forcibly removed from their homes. The promise was to employ 6,000 workers in an impoverished part of the city. The plant was built, but under Roger Smith's push for more automation, it opened with only half the promised workforce.[12]

For Barra, it was a chance to run something on her own and prove herself. It was also a crappy assignment. The plant had low quality. The cars it made, the big Cadillac Seville and DeVille and Buick LeSabre sedans, were boulevard boats of a bygone era. Luxury buyers wanted sporty cars from Mercedes and BMW. They wanted crossover SUVs from Lexus, not big DeVilles. Those cars were for the parents of luxury buyers and retirees in Boca Raton.

Barra had to go in and slow down the assembly lines to match production with slowing sales. That meant layoffs. But she didn't just cut to the bone. The plant kept enough people so Barra could slow the line and still produce enough cars to meet targets. With a slower line, fewer mistakes were made, so quality improved. That meant the workers didn't need to spend as much time fixing gaffes later, so productivity eventually improved, too. She also organized the work crews into small teams of five or six people. They had team leaders helping to coordinate the work. If employees found problems, they had direct access to someone who could help. Line workers felt more involved in the process.

"She cut a lot of jobs, but put it this way, she's the head so everything falls on her good or bad," said George McGregor, a shop committeeman for Local 22, which represented the factory's workers. "She was high on quality. She was a pretty good leader and people person."

The changes helped quality, and in 2005, J.D. Power gave the plant its first-ever quality award with a first place for the LeSabre. Cowger was impressed, and Barra was on her way to bigger things.

CHAPTER 3

BARRA AND BANKRUPTCY

Barra's success at Hamtramck vaulted her into upper management. Cowger, GM's North America president, promoted her to executive director of global manufacturing engineering in 2004. From her new job, Barra had a front-row seat during one of the most tumultuous times in the company's history.

She would help Cowger get plants ready to make new models and, more important, undertake his plan to boost productivity and quality. He wanted GM to use the same machines and processes the world over, which Toyota had been doing for years. It was a big part of CEO Rick Wagoner's plan to fix the problems he could most easily control, like the appeal of GM's vehicles, quality, and productivity.

Wagoner had already brought in Bob Lutz, the legendary car guy who had come up with BMW's Ultimate Driving Machine marketing moniker and who turned Chrysler's Dodge Ram pickup into a legitimate contender against Ford and Chevy in the lucrative truck market. He also had a hand with hit cars like the Chrysler 300M and growth of the Jeep line. At GM, he oversaw product development when the company had hits with the Cadillac Escalade SUV and CTS sedan, as well as the seventh-generation Chevy Malibu, which put GM back on the map with family sedan buyers.

With Lutz sprucing up the product line and Cowger and Barra trying to fix manufacturing, Wagoner could focus on a huge problem for which GM had no easy fix: how to pay for the healthcare benefits for 270,000 retirees and their dependents. In all, GM was covering medical costs for 1 million people, which gave the company that cost penalty of $1,600 for every car it sold. It was crippling. It all but guaranteed that GM couldn't make money on small cars and most family sedans, which were thinly profitable at most car companies. Like the other Detroit automakers, GM made most of its money on pickup trucks, SUVs, and the GMAC auto lending business. Much of its lineup lost money year in, year out.

Wagoner's solution was to try to grow the business with Lutz's cars, improve margins with the work Cowger and Barra were doing, and slug it out until the actuarial tables turned in his favor.[1] That is to say, wait for retirees to start dying off, taking the cost bogey with them.

The nuts-and-bolts part of the plan was showing progress. In product development, Lutz had given designers a bigger voice. Cars looked better and the cabins felt richer, even in the Chevy cars. Before Lutz got there, GM's interiors were notoriously cheap. Market share had stabilized to about 28 percent through 2004 and the trucks and SUVs were selling well. GM made $3.8 billion in 2003 and $2.8 billion in 2004. That was a fraction of Toyota's profits, but a crisis seemed far off.

GM had routinely been a laggard in studies like J.D. Power's Initial Quality Study in the 1990s, but improvements made in the vehicles and plants in 2004 would show up in results the next year, when four of its brands ranked average or better. Bread-and-butter Chevy and luxury Cadillac both finished in the top third. Again, it wasn't Toyota, but it was a respectable finish.

Barra's job was to lead manufacturing engineering to design every plant so it would work the same, and build vehicles designed for, say, Europe, in a plant in the US or Mexico. Since the company was built through a series of acquisitions going back 100 years, engineers and workers did things differently everywhere. It led to all kinds of redundant engineering and waste. It also made quality tough to fix because plants often had different processes and equipment. It was hard to send out best practices when many factories did things differently.

While Toyota's Corolla compact and Honda's Civic mostly used the same parts the world over, GM had many different small cars. Cowger said the company was building one version of the Opel Corsa compact in its home market in Europe, another in Brazil, and a third one in Mexico. And the Chevy Cobalt sold in the US was also different from those.

"I was trying to commonize it in Mexico and found out they were basically different cars," Cowger said.

One of the worst examples was the Saturn L-series, GM's effort to sell a family sedan with its cheery compact-car brand. In 2000, the company took the Opel Vectra midsized car and modified it for what was thought to be American consumer tastes, then they sent it to a plant in Wilmington, Delaware, to be built.

It challenged the assembly line. Things like door handles and other key parts didn't fit and had to be modified. Part of that was a result of different plants and engineering, and part was because the managers in Europe and the US wanted so many unique things for their respective markets that commonality went by the wayside. The car didn't sell well. Saturn lost $1 billion in a single year largely because of the sales shortfalls and cost overruns to produce the L-series, *Business-Week* reported in 2003.[2] The car was canceled in 2005.

With the work Barra and Cowger were doing, productivity had improved, though. In 2005, GM had three of the five most productive plants in North America, according to the Harbour Report,[3] an industry study that measures how many labor hours each model took to build. The company also had the most productive engine plant and the best stamping facility, which presses out steel body panels.

The next year, it got even better. GM needed just over thirty-two hours of labor to make a vehicle, which was best of the domestic automakers and less than two hours' more time than leaders Toyota and Nissan. Five years earlier, the difference had been six hours, the Harbour report said.

GM could have slogged it out that way for years making incremental improvements under the burden of $70 billion in retiree healthcare liabilities and an equally huge pension fund, but disaster was already brewing. Economic growth in Asia—especially China, where GM's Buick brand was popular and growing—was also pushing up demand for oil. Supply wasn't keeping up. By August of 2004, oil had hit $60 a barrel and wasn't settling down. Gasoline prices rose to $1.90. Car buyers were starting to slowly migrate away from bigger vehicles.

That summer I went to the Woodward Dream Cruise, an annual celebration of muscle cars, horsepower, and carbon exhaust that starts on Woodward Avenue in downtown Detroit and runs thirty miles to Pontiac. Wagoner was on hand at an event about twelve miles from downtown on Woodward with a dozen new copies of the Chevy SSR, a limited-edition model that looked like the love child of a pickup truck and a hot rod with a 390-horsepower V-8 that got fifteen miles to the gallon. I asked Wagoner if higher gasoline prices had crimped his pickup and SUV sales.

"We haven't seen it having an effect so far," he said at the time.

It was coming. Before long, dealers would be discounting gas guzzlers to keep sales going. In a column for *BusinessWeek* under the headline "Detroit Is Over a ($50) Barrel,"[4] the magazine pointed out that Detroit's carmakers were keeping gas guzzler sales moving with rebates and other deals that cost an average of $6,000 a vehicle. "They're overcoming the fuel-cost increase with incentives that you can't believe," Detroit-area Chevy dealer Gordon Stewart told me at the time.

While GM was showing off the SSR, Toyota was boosting production of its fifty-mile-per-gallon Prius and a hybrid-electric version of its Lexus RX 330 SUV. Honda was getting ready to sell its third hybrid vehicle, an Accord family sedan that combined 240 horses with thirty miles a gallon.

Two different public relations people at GM sent emails, and one was the most scathing letter I had ever received. It got personal, accusing me of being just another biased reporter who loved the Japanese cars and carmakers and had it in for GM. (I've never owned a Japanese vehicle.) The other was less livid but still dismissive. He said he'd call me to talk about how wrong I was if I would listen, but if I won't hear him out then he wouldn't bother. We had a pretty good conversation. He said GM would absolutely be able to react to higher fuel prices by switching over to more efficient models and still make money.

He was wrong. By the middle of 2005, oil prices crossed $80 a barrel. Gasoline prices went higher than $2.50. Consumers started fleeing SUVs and pickup trucks for smaller models, which the Japanese were better at selling. Since GM made most of its money with those models, the year would be a bloodbath.

GM sales fell 5 percent in the first quarter and the company posted a $1.1 billion loss. Wagoner suspended guidance to Wall Street analysts, which was the equivalent to saying that he didn't know when the bleeding would stop. The company was also burning cash.

This was a crucial point in the company's history. GM had, for years, denied that its cars were dull, refused to address its quality issues, and had never found a way to give all of its brands distinction. Under Wagoner, GM was trying to mend itself. He was making progress with some long-standing problems. What he couldn't easily fix was the massive amount of debt and retiree obligations that were choking the company. Those retiree obligations and the debt GM took on to pay them off meant that no matter how hard people like Barra worked to fix decades-old problems, a serious recession would shove the company into a full-blown crisis. From 1993 to 2008, GM had paid $105 billion in pension and healthcare costs, Wagoner said.

In 2005, the GM narrative was beginning to sound like O. Henry's "The Cop and the Anthem," in which Soapy the bum tries to get arrested to spend the cold winter in jail. When he decides to turn his life around, he is arrested for loitering. GM spent decades denying its worst problems. Right when the company started to fix them, an economic crisis hit and the company wasn't ready.

That fuel price spike hit the company hard. Oil prices would stay elevated all year. GM's SUV sales fell 30 percent, and the largest and most profitable of them, the Chevy Suburban, Cadillac Escalade, and GMC Yukon, dropped the most. The company lost $8.6 billion in 2005, its second biggest loss ever. Wagoner called it "one of the most difficult years in GM's history." He started by closing nine plants and cutting 34,000 workers[5] with a target of cutting at least $6 billion in costs.

That year, *BusinessWeek* ran a cover story with the ominous title, "Why GM's Plan Won't Work and the Ugly Road

Ahead." In the nine-page special report, the magazine predicted that without some kind of serious intervention, the company would end up in bankruptcy. It had too many workers, too many brands to support, and the debt and retiree costs were more than any company could handle.

The harsh conclusion was that GM needed a reckoning just to survive. Wagoner would have to get the union to give in on jobs and the Jobs Bank, which was an old contract clause that forced Detroit's automakers to pay laid-off workers 95 percent of their pay to do nothing, often for years. The UAW would also have to agree to cut retiree benefits. Management would have to stop perpetuating itself and chop four of its eight brands, maybe get rid of Buick, Pontiac, Hummer, and Saab. And its dealers would have to live with it instead of demanding big payouts to go away, as they did when the company spent $1 billion to cut ties with 2,800 Oldsmobile dealers in 2000.

That cover story, which ran in May 2005, predicted that a recession would force GM into bankruptcy. With market share falling, the company no longer had the critical mass to cover its costs and fund new models and technology. Wagoner's plan to use Lutz's new models, which were a vast improvement, was hamstrung by one difficult fact. With its cash constraints, GM was freshening its models less frequently than its competitors. Toyota and Honda replaced an aging vehicle with a fresh version every five years. GM did it every seven. Fresh models almost always win with consumers. No matter how much creativity Lutz unleashed from GM's many talented designers and engineers, or how efficient the plants were, the company was always chasing the game.

Barra was part of the restructuring plan since GM had to cut workers and get its production in line with demand. She was also helping Cowger develop factories overseas to find growth. GM may have been a mess at home, but in China the Buick brand was hot and sales grew 32 percent. For the first time in the company's history, more than half of its sales came from outside the US.

That growth, plus cost cuts, helped GM make a $2.2 billion adjusted profit in 2006. But adding back restructuring costs and other charges, the company lost $2 billion. It was an improvement, but CFO Frederick "Fritz" Henderson was quick to point out that GM had a lot of work to do.

"I would say no one's declaring victory, though, at this point at General Motors. Nobody," Henderson said after announcing earnings for the year.

Going into 2008, most of GM's plants were finally aligned with the GM-S manufacturing system Cowger and Barra were installing. The plants were building vehicles in a similar way using common parts with the workers doing things the same way. They were building four new plants in China, Russia, and India. GM opened a new one in San Luis Potosi, Mexico, to feed vehicles to the US market. All of those plants were opened in 2008.

"We were making a lot of progress fixing the company's problems," said Cowger.

It was too late. If the oil price spike was a gut punch, the financial crisis brought the company to its knees. Subprime lenders started going bankrupt in 2007. When Lehman Brothers collapsed in the fall of 2008, the banking system was in full-blown meltdown. Lending froze. Business activity seized up. Unemployment rose from a chilling 9.5 percent in 2007 to a depressionary 13.2 percent in 2008, and auto sales tumbled to their lowest level since 1992. Without car loans, sales ground to a halt. Americans would buy a paltry 13 million vehicles that year, down from more than 16 million in 2007.

"In my view, what happened in 2009, this complete lack of liquidity in the financial markets, has never happened in modern history," Wagoner told me years later. "The government response to Covid, as compared to 2009, was radically different. The House and Senate approved funding urgently. The Fed worked radically, providing funding support to the markets. Had they worked that quickly in 2009, that would have helped tremendously."

As much restructuring as GM had done and as much growth as they were getting overseas, and despite all the work that dedicated executives like Barra were doing, nothing could stop what was coming. With sales cratering, GM and Chrysler were on the brink of bankruptcy. Ford had borrowed almost $24 billion in 2006, mortgaging every asset including the Ford blue oval logo to get the money. The company had cash to survive as the financial crisis wreaked havoc on Main Street America.

Wagoner and Chrysler CEO Bob Nardelli went to Washington for congressional hearings. Their plea was that the companies would run out of cash without a government infusion and that the blow to the US economy would be too much to bear.

George W. Bush, who was a lame duck and due to turn the keys to the Oval Office over to Barack Obama the next month, approved $17.4 billion to keep the two companies afloat, but they would have to return in February to make a case to the Obama administration to continue funding both companies once that money ran out.

Barra was on the team working on the restructuring plans that would satisfy the Treasury Department and get GM another slug of cash to survive long enough to downsize the company. It was night after night of late hours with Wagoner, Henderson, GM's former head of government affairs and now US representative Debbie Dingell, and others. They were working with investment bankers Dan Ammann, who was with Morgan Stanley, and Evercore's Stephen Worth, among others, said John Smith, who was overseeing product planning and strategy.

The team was cloistered in a sweaty, stinky conference room on the thirty-seventh floor. The thirty-eighth and thirty-ninth floors were the top executive offices and closed off by security. Everyone had access to thirty-seven so it was convenient. They subsisted on company pantry coffee and takeout while trying to figure out how GM would survive.

"Me and my team are in the conference room twenty hours a day taking everybody's comments in," said Smith. "Mary was at that point Gary Cowger's chief manufacturing planning person. We were having to go through and figure out what's the company going to look like if we have an out-of-court restructuring or an in-court restructuring."

The latter is a corporate euphemism for bankruptcy. The team was looking at which plants would be kept and how many people would stay on, Smith said. In the early months of 2009, they were working on a second restructuring report. The Treasury Department wanted GM to take a sharper pencil to cutting weak vehicles models. Behind every one of those cars that would be cut is an assembly plant, engine and transmission plants, and jobs. Barra was in the thick of it.

"It was all about assembly plants and people," Smith said. "There I would say it was a weekly occurrence where Fritz would say we have to take another $500 million out of the engineering budget or capex budget. That probably happened five or six times."

When Henderson asked for deeper cuts, Barra and her team would have to figure out what that meant in terms of metal stamping, or engine and assembly plants. And she was always looking to see how she could help, Smith recalls.

"Mary would frequently stop by the conference room, notwithstanding the odors that were coming from it from twenty-hour days with stale food," Smith said. "She would poke her head in wondering what more she could do. That's classic Mary."

Barra's knowledge of GM's factory network came in handy as the company cut out four of its brands—Hummer, Pontiac, Saab, and Saturn—and laid off 47,000 workers.

"Think about her background," Smith said. "She started in the trenches of GM at age seventeen or eighteen in the plants seeing how this choreography of men, materials, and machines work together. She came up right through the ranks in the earthiest part of our business."

At the first hearing in February, Wagoner and Nardelli made a renewed plea for more government assistance. But they didn't offer a plan for how they would cut down debt and have enough to pay the government back. GM just said it would need as much as $16.6 billion just to survive. The company's plan did call for eliminating cutting about 20 percent of its workforce and ditching four of its eight brands.

The Obama administration wasn't satisfied. In late March, the Treasury Department gave GM tough love, telling Wagoner to slash some of GM's $62 billion in total debt. The Task Force, led by investment banker Steve Rattner, wanted GM to get its bondholders to take a haircut and accept $9.2 billion instead of the $27.5 billion they were owed. Likewise, GM needed to get the union to accept half the $20 billion GM planned to give them for a fund to cover retiree healthcare. They had sixty days to do it.

Days later, the Treasury Department's Auto Task Force shocked the business world by ousting Wagoner as CEO and putting COO Henderson in charge. Wagoner had been opposed to filing for bankruptcy protection. He worried that consumers would never buy a car from a bankrupt GM for fear that the company wouldn't be around to honor warranties. He thought it would be the end of the company.

When I had written four years earlier that GM would likely end up in bankruptcy, his response to the story was, "Anyone who thinks we can solve our problems by filing for bankruptcy doesn't understand our business."

The Treasury Department's Auto Task Force and GM's board were going to name Henderson the interim CEO. He pleaded with them not to tag him as "interim," because if they did people at the company would ignore him. That's just part of the culture. So they made him CEO, though he knew he had little chance of lasting out the year in the job.

Armageddon came on June 1. The culmination of losing more than half its market share since Barra was born and bleeding $88 billion in red ink since 2004 left the company with no choice. The only saving grace was that the federal government would shepherd GM through an expedited bankruptcy, guaranteeing with bridge loans and cash to preserve warranties, keep parts coming in, and workers paid so GM might survive.

The government set up what was called a "363 sale" in which the company would sell the assets it wanted to keep to a "new GM" and leave some old assets behind, the carcass of "old GM," that creditors would fight over to recoup any portion of the debt that wasn't paid. Old GM was basically a junk bucket of defunct factories, real estate, and, importantly, some financial and legal liabilities.

For Barra, the filing was a time of reflection. She had worked with Cowger to improve GM's plants and, years before, with Harry Pearce to examine the company's culture. But with bankruptcy came a time to wonder if it was worth staying. She had considered leaving the company at that point, she told me in an interview. But she stuck around to see the crisis through.

Why stick it out? Barra said that she stayed because of a pride in the company and a desire to make it work, to ensure that there would be a GM left for some of the talented and hardworking people that dedicated their lives to it.

"I'm proud of GM. My dad was very proud of the company," she said. "The reason I stayed and the reason I believed is that the people of GM are so incredibly talented and hardworking."

Perseverance often pays off. Sticking around created major opportunities. A lot of executives had moved on. Wagoner was out and North America president Troy Clarke left. So did Katy Barclay, who had been Wagoner's head of human resources.

Henderson tapped Barra as head of HR. Here she was again, an engineer, being shoehorned into a soft discipline far from her expertise. He said it made sense because the Treasury Department wanted to see culture change. Barra knew what was wrong both in management and engineering ranks and on the plant floor. She had great insights.

"Mary knew how slow it was," Henderson told me. "I thought she could move the needle in that way. She knew the norms and knew which executives aren't performing well and have not been dealt with. I felt she could do that."

Once she was a VP, Barra went about trying to simplify GM. One thing she did, humorously, was replace a lengthy dress code at the company with two words. "Dress appropriately." Barra said later that she didn't think people needed to wear suits, ties, or dresses, but professionals also should know how to look when they get to the office.

The dress code implied that you came to work in a shirt and tie unless you worked in a plant. For a while that changed to casual Fridays, which at GM meant a nice pair of pants, sports coat, and no tie. That soon drifted to jeans on Friday. Then someone would come in with holes in their jeans and some manager would raise the issue. Mary was trying to change the culture of rules and regulations at GM and pushing individuals to make smart decisions on their own, said John Quattrone, who worked in HR for Barra.

"Business was changing. People were not wearing ties anymore," Quattrone said. "People want instruction. The team was coming up with rules. OK, jeans on Friday and other rules. And Mary replaced the code with two words."

Henderson also tried to speed up decision making by slimming down the star chamber of top executives who met on big decisions. He replaced Wagoner's Automotive Strategy Board, which had more than twenty members, and the Automotive Product Board with just one group of nine managers including himself.

He also retired out some longtime company managers. GM North American president Troy Clarke and Barra's old boss Gary Cowger retired. So did Maureen Kempston Darkes, who ran GM's Latin American business, and Mike Grimaldi, who oversaw GM's joint venture in Korea.

The slim chance Henderson had of keeping the CEO's job evaporated at the December 2009 board meeting. Half the board of directors were there for the first time. Henderson opened saying, "OK, well, this will open a new chapter," and he started talking about the current condition of the company, Akerson recalled in an interview.

"I said, 'Whoa, don't you think we should have had a pre-board meeting?'" Akerson shot back. "Tell us, 'This is what's right, this is what's wrong, here are the deficient areas.'"

Akerson and private equity investor/GM board member David Bonderman were tough and critical during the meeting.

They and other board members, like retired Coke CEO Neville Isdell, wanted an assessment of GM's problems and a detailed plan to fix them. Henderson and CFO Ray Young didn't have enough detail. The board decided to send Fritz to an early retirement. He didn't even get a pension. Henderson told me the only benefit he gets is a GM car.

The board did a "semi search," as non-executive chairman Ed Whitacre described it to me. "But we didn't have much luck," he said.

In Henderson's place, the board put Whitacre in just a few weeks later. The tall, laconic Texan was already past retirement age but took the helm at GM to stabilize the business and bring about culture change while the board searched for a long-term leader.

He held a conference call with top managers to explain what was happening. Some of them asked if he wanted their resignations. Whitacre was clear that he had good people at the top of the house, and told them, "I can't do this without you."[6]

He did ease out a handful of executives, though. One of them was Lutz. At seventy-three, he was well past retirement age and his ego had rubbed new board members the wrong way. So, too, did his macho, cigar-smoking, sports-car-driving ways. The board also saw him as very old Detroit, Isdell said in an interview.

Whitacre liked Reuss and Barra. He thought Reuss had engineering smarts and passion for the business. He said Barra was smart and also a good person. He also sensed early on that, despite being a GM lifer, she knew how screwed up its management culture was and how overwrought and slow the decision process was.

"She knew instinctively that there were problems," Whitacre said. "I knew she had a lot of ability. I saw CEO potential."

Whitacre had a habit of walking into meetings, sometimes unannounced, and asking if the people in the room knew why they were even having the meeting. He met with his senior staff just once a week. He also cut the metrics by which he measured managers from twelve to six core numbers: market share, revenue, operating profit, cash flow, quality, and customer satisfaction.

Since Barra was head of human resources, she had access to a lot of data. Whitacre decided to have her face off with the Treasury Department on the company's performance and to argue with paymaster Kenneth Feinberg over how much the company could pay executives. With the government owning a stake in GM, the company had to keep executive pay capped at $500,000 a year. Whitacre also had to retain and hire talent on what corporate America would see as meager pay.

Feinberg said it wasn't an argument at all. That isn't Barra's style. True to form, she won him over with humility and a sensible plan. Feinberg's job was to determine what the top twenty-five executives would be paid. It had to stay within strict federal rules, and fat-cat perks were not allowed.

While insurance giant American International Group CEO Bob Benmosche drove a hard bargain and claimed his top managers would all split for better pay from competitors and even the Chinese, Barra was a team player. At an opening meeting between the two, she told Feinberg that GM and its management pay rates were a drop in the bucket compared to what AIG and big Wall Street banks were paying.

"She was fabulous," Feinberg said. "She said, 'Ken, we are in a certain sense an afterthought. We are not BofA, AIG, or Citibank. Our top twenty-five executives at GM, if you combine annual compensation, it's less than the top two or three at BofA or Citi. We're out of bankruptcy. We're moving forward.

We have a plan. Keep in mind we don't have salaries, bonuses, and perks the way some of the other companies do.'"

It was not a case of "as GM goes so goes the country," Feinberg recalls Barra telling him.

She told Feinberg that GM wasn't going to fight the Feds. Then she submitted a plan that was within the bounds of the law and offered executives compensation over time, with stock awards and other instruments that would enrich them later, once GM showed that it could grow post-bankruptcy.

As for perks and the kind of largesse that GM used to dole out in the pre-bankruptcy years such as company planes, Barra said, "We don't have perks anymore."

Whitacre liked her, too. She had no ego and wasn't afraid of a new boss. When he arrived on the heels of the firing of two CEOs, people feared him. He said he would go down to the food court in the lower level of the company's Renaissance Center headquarters—five shiny towers on the Detroit River—and people would walk in the other direction.

"You'd have thought I had black plague," Whitacre told me.

Not Barra. She and her husband, Tony, whom she met in college at GMI, asked Whitacre to dinner. Barra was the only executive to do so. That's where he got to know her vision for GM.

"I came away from that discussion in a different place," Whitacre said. "She's passionate about it. She wanted to make GM great again."

At that time, Whitacre was preparing GM to go public. He had hired Microsoft Corporation's CFO Chris Liddell for the same job at GM. Akerson, who was chair of the board's audit committee, had been cleaning up the books.

The IPO would be a rebirth for GM. It would bring the company's shares back to the public markets and enable the Treasury Department to eventually get out of owning businesses.

That would help GM shed the "Government Motors" label that bedeviled its reputation with consumers, some of whom saw that bailout as the coup de grace that proved GM's longstanding inferiority. The Obama administration also wanted to be out of GM as fast as possible in order to shed the socialist label coming from right-wing critics.

But this is GM. Nothing happens without drama. Just days before the company would file the paperwork for an initial public offering, Whitacre quit. At sixty-nine, he had no intention of going through an exhausting road show or running GM for some time after. Since a big part of an IPO is telling investors how good management is, the board needed to find a replacement and fast.

So, in August 2010, with no internal candidates ready and few outsiders interested in the job, the board hired one of its own, Dan Akerson. A hard-boiled former Navy man who went into private equity, Akerson was all about discipline. He was appalled at the time it took to get things done at GM and the state of the books and finances when he ran the board's audit committee.

Since GM had been run by finance guys for decades, the accounting and reporting should have been squeaky clean. Akerson thought the books were a mess. He found that the company had four different ledgers. Big corporations typically have one. Before bankruptcy, GM was often running right up against deadline to file its annual report. When it filed for bankruptcy, it had four material weaknesses in its financial reporting. Companies usually have at most one. There were also a dozen deficiencies, Akerson said.

The company also outsourced its IT and didn't have control over its own data. That made it hard to figure out where it was making and losing money in its far-flung global operations. GM was too big and didn't have the controls in place to keep track of all of its businesses. Akerson brought IT in-house and later had Ammann improve internal controls.

With Akerson in charge, GM would get a cultural shake-up. And Barra's career would get supercharged. He liked her immensely. Plus, when a board feels it has to name one of its own as CEO, it says that the field for the next chief executive is wide open. And it was. The house cleaning that happened during bankruptcy would give Barra an open look at top jobs and a real chance to run the business.

CHAPTER 4

⚡

BARRA'S RISE AND THE FIRST ELECTRIC PUSH

Dan Akerson took over GM in September of 2010. Shortly after taking the job, he called Barra to his office for a meeting.

"I asked her, 'What the hell are you doing in human resources?'"

Akerson thought that an electrical engineer who had run a factory, played a key role in leaning up GM's inefficient network of plants, and had helped restructure the manufacturing operations during bankruptcy was woefully underemployed in HR. He had big plans for her and thought she was someone he could trust as he worked to rip up what he saw as a fat-cat culture that GM executives had enjoyed for decades, even as the company's performance declined.

He told me that the HR appointment was "a weak attempt to get her more rounded out."

A graduate of the US Naval Academy and the London School of Economics, Akerson could be blunt as a night stick and brooked no bullshit. He was a boxer at Annapolis and no less pugnacious atop GM. He came to the automaker's board from private equity giant Carlyle Group, the D.C. financier famed for its political connections. The firm had George H.W.

Bush, former secretary of state James Baker and former British prime minister John Major as advisors in the late 1990s. Federal Reserve Chairman Jerome Powell has also done a turn at the private equity giant.

Before Carlyle, Akerson ran General Instrument and later MCI and was successful at both companies. He took over GM as a matter of noblesse oblige. He took his lumps, too, having been CEO of XO Communications when it went bankrupt in 2002. Akerson told me that he felt guilty for years that he had left the Navy after serving the minimum five years he owed for his education. His father was also a Navy man. Though he had made millions, he candidly describes himself as nouveau riche and felt he had to give something back to the nation. He figured being admiral of GM through the uncertain waters of its post-bankruptcy years was a way to do it.

He often ran GM like a crew of midshipmen. Engineers in product development griped that he had one lever to pull as a manager: give 'em hell. Some needed it, but there were plenty of GM lifers who, like Barra, knew the company was lumbering and complacent and wanted to fix it. They didn't need a kick up the backside. What they wanted was someone to cut through the bureaucracy. They also thought he didn't understand why it took four years to develop a vehicle because he didn't know the reality that it takes four years to get factories to make the 30,000 parts that make up an automobile.

When I told him what some of the veterans thought, he replied, "They thought I pushed them too hard? Too bad. I'm doing what I thought was best for the company."

That's Akerson. GM had a lot of smart people, but overall the company did require a cultural enema and he was determined to do it. He wanted to replace entitlement and complacency with discipline and urgency.

When he got into the executive offices on the thirty-ninth floor, he noticed that the round corridor to the top offices was lined with portraits of CEOs going back to GM founder Billy Durant. GM would have a portrait of each CEO painted after they retired. He hated it.

"It's like the dead white men's club," Akerson said. "In my opinion, most of them were failures."

After taking the job, Akerson met with Wagoner to talk all things GM. He said he was dismayed that Wagoner asked him when his portrait would be up. He had them all taken down except for Durant's and Alfred Sloan's and replaced them with pictures of GM's cars.

During his first winter in the job, Akerson said he noticed small flies buzzing around his office. There he was in the dead of Michigan winter, thirty-nine floors above the city with midwestern gales swirling around the towers and ice chunks floating in the Detroit River, and he had flies. He asked the secretary what gives, and she said it's from the executive showers. Some executive offices had their own large bathroom, a shower, and even a large comfortable chair for reading. She said she would have the bathrooms cleaned.

Akerson wanted them gone. He moved his office down a few floors to the eighteenth floor so his direct reports could come in and see him without going through security on the thirty-ninth floor. Then he told GM's facilities people to get rid of the private bathrooms and remodel the top floor for more office space. He was told it would cost $18 million.

"I said, 'Find someone who will do it for $3 million or I'll find someone who will,'" Akerson said. "It was like nothing I'd ever seen before. I gutted the whole floor."

He figured less opulence would bring about a more workmanlike mentality. When it was done, executives were sharing bathrooms, offices were smaller, and there were LCD screens that showed GM's share price and social media comments about its cars and brands. The executive dining room was changed to serve cold cuts and warm soup.

As Akerson pushed for a tougher mentality, he felt that Barra really got it. Akerson told Barra he wanted her to take over product development. She was interested in the job, but first asked what was to become of the man who was in the job.

"What about Tom Stephens?" he recalls her asking.

Stephens had been with GM for forty years. He was the archetypal Detroit car guy. He grew up with a wrench in his hand and earned his stripes in GM's powertrain operations. That is, developing engines and transmissions. At home, he collected Motor City metal, surrounding himself with such gems of brawny Americana as 1966, '67, '70, and '74 Corvettes, a '70 Buick Grand Sport, a '66 Chevy Chevelle, a '79 Pontiac Trans Am, and a '64 Pontiac GTO, he told Ward'sAuto.[1] Stephens was also devoutly loyal to GM.

Akerson liked Stephens but said he was caught in a time warp. He was simply too old school for a company that had to prove to consumers that it could overcome its dinosaur past. Akerson bemoaned that Stephens had his secretary print out emails a few times a day rather than read them himself and reply instantly. That frustrated Akerson, who thought the entire company moved too slowly. So he called Stephens into his office and told him he would name him vice chairman and make him an advisor to the CEO, but Barra would run the group.

"I knew I was killing him," Akerson said, adding that, "Tom was set in old ways. You need your best people in the toughest jobs. And I wanted someone with a fresh look."

That move punched through the glass ceiling and accelerated Barra's career. No auto company ever had a woman leading new-car development. Stephens was a true motorhead. Lutz, his predecessor, was an ex-Marine pilot who loved his cigars, gin martinis, had his own collection of classic cars, and even flew his own fighter jet. In very different ways, they both embodied the macho spirit of Detroit car guys.

Barra's promotion shook GM to its core. Internally, engineers and designers were flummoxed. She didn't have the reputation of Lutz and had not grown up in vehicle engineering like Stephens. One veteran designer commented to me at the time that they knew very little about Barra. She had been in manufacturing and human resources but had been nowhere near engineering work or design decisions. Another commented to me that, far from being a visionary, some of the men in engineering saw her as "a capable administrator." Compliments don't get much more backhanded than that.

Not all of the criticism was unfair at the time. She came from HR. No one likes the HR department in any company, and at that point it had been her biggest job. But "capable administrator" would not accurately describe Barra as she climbed the ladder. Under Cowger, she had worked to standardize manufacturing around the world and had a role in opening plants in Russia and India. She also ran the D-Ham plant and walked the floor with union workers.

When she got into the product development role, one of the first things she did was press hard to take out layers of management and streamline decision making. At GM, every vehicle program had what was called a vehicle line executive, or VLE, on top, with a chief engineer, designers, and all kinds of support staff for each manager on every model. Some vehicles even had their own public relations person just for a couple of cars. Barra wanted to have managers oversee multiple vehicles, which would give them more responsibility and also reduce the support staff underneath them.

She picked John Quattrone as her head of human resources to help slim the place down. They had worked closely together in HR previously. Quattrone is a wisecracking, no-BS guy who grew up in hardscrabble Syracuse, New York. He saw that GM had always had too many managers and too many layers that cost the company time and money.

"We had too many senior executives," Quattrone said. "We wanted to skinny the organization down."

Barra did it humanely, Quattrone said. But she wanted fewer people and to make the remaining managers more accountable. They didn't want managers with one or two direct reports. Everyone should have nine or ten, he said. She cut out many of those jobs and organized the company under vehicle platform teams. There would be an executive chief engineer overseeing, say, large trucks or midsized SUVs. The vehicles within that family would have engineers and designers, but it eliminated redundant bosses and the posse of people each one often had.

"We didn't kill anyone. We had early retirements," Quattrone said. "We took out significant cost."

During Barra's time heading product development, a lot of her focus was on cutting cost and getting vehicles to market faster. Akerson had challenged her with that task both because the company still needed to get leaner and because he wanted to see if she could be tough and take an axe to GM's old ways. The board was also pressing GM to become nimbler.

"She was really working on the innards and getting them straight and simplified," said retired GM board member Isdell. "One thing was, how do we get to market quicker? There were all sorts of things that derailed speeding them up. We were looking at how to shorten time to market. GM was too slow in that arena."

GM did get the Chevrolet Colorado and GMC Canyon small pickups out quickly. Whitacre had ordered them up in late 2010, saying that in his home state of Texas young people would love a smaller, cheaper truck. By 2013, Chevy was showing the new model off at the Los Angeles Auto Show, and dealers were selling them by mid-2014. It wasn't light speed, but the project was done in less than four years, and since Ford had stopped selling the Ranger in the US, GM found itself with a hit truck and a market all to itself.

Barra had a big hand in developing GM's first real push to compete in electric vehicles. When she started the job, GM was selling the Chevy Volt, a compact car that ran on electric power but had a gasoline engine on board to recharge the battery if it got too low. In 2010, when it went on sale, charging stations were tough to find. Road trips were almost impossible for EV owners unless they wanted to plan a special route and go out of their way to find a place to charge up. And back then, charging took hours.

The Volt was a pragmatic effort originally spearheaded by Lutz to leapfrog Toyota's Prius. And technologically it did. The Prius got extra boost from its electric motor to save gasoline. A Volt could drive thirty-five miles on its electric battery alone, which was enough to get 70 percent of commuters to work and back each day without burning a drop of gas. That first-generation Volt had an Apple-inspired dashboard, too. Touch the slick white plastic and you could control the HVAC, audio, and other functions.

When GM started working on the second-generation Volt, Akerson and Barra pushed the team to reduce the losses on the car, which were as high as $16,000 for every vehicle sold. The second-generation car used more parts and structural pieces from the Chevy Cruze compact to save money. It had a better battery and could go fifty-three miles on a charge before the gasoline engine kicked in to charge the battery pack.

GM designers had been working on a variety of possible vehicles using the Volt's gasoline-electric system. All of them would lose money, but they could broaden appeal for plug-in cars. There was a midsized crossover SUV that designers had been working on. Consumers were buying more and more crossovers because they drove better than huge SUVs but had a lot of cabin space and storage. A plug-in version would have been more popular than a compact like the Volt. Americans have rarely embraced compact cars.

It wasn't to be. Akerson had challenged Barra to cut costs and make the product development work more profitable. Adding more money-losing plug-ins wasn't a way to do that. He was already pushing the team to take $10,000 a vehicle in cost out of the existing Volt so GM could reduce losses while also dropping the sticker price and boosting sales. Bigger sales would drive acceptance of the new technology and help lower battery costs. After a few years of work, GM greatly reduced the losses on the Volt, said Tony Posawatz, a former GM engineer who ran the Volt program.

GM produced the Cadillac ELR. It was a sporty two-door version of the Volt that was more about performance driving than cutting emissions. The first Volt had 149 horsepower while the ELR ran on a zippier 233-hp system. The car was still highly efficient, but luxury buyers don't like small vehicles and two-door coupes are a small niche. It didn't sell very well.

What the Volt and ELR did do was reestablish GM's push into electric drive. To get the Volt project going, the company had to scour its own ranks for veterans of the EV1 and other hybrid-electric vehicle programs that the company had during the previous decade, Posawatz said.

GM still thought that the Volt powertrain was a great compromise at the time. It gave drivers the security that they would never be stranded with a discharged battery. As long as a Volt driver could find a gas station, they could keep driving. Posawatz even coined the phrase "range anxiety" to describe how car buyers worried about buying electric cars due to a dearth of places to charge.

Still, with Tesla making noise about pure electric vehicles and Nissan selling its Leaf, GM had been pondering an electric car. The Chinese government was pressing automakers to build "New Energy Vehicles," which were plug-in hybrids like the Volt or pure EVs.

In 2010, GM's vice chairman, Stephen Girsky, got a call from Juno Chung, COO of Korean battery maker LG Chem. They met for dinner at Coach Insignia, a restaurant at the top of GM's Renaissance Center headquarters that rotated to give diners a panoramic view of downtown Detroit, the Detroit River, and Windsor, Ontario. Chung wanted to build an electric car with GM.

His pitch: LG would supply the battery and pay for part of the car's development. Since GM was still getting on its feet financially and electric cars lose money, Girsky figured why not?

"I said I'm willing to listen because these things financially aren't that good," Girsky told me.

Now came the hard part, getting GM's product development organization to embrace the idea. GM's engineers had been notoriously resistant to working with other companies and relinquishing control. There was also a lot of resistance to making a pure electric vehicle. GM lost more than $1 billion on the EV1 and took a very public black eye for discontinuing the project. Many GM engineers didn't think the car-buying public was ready for pure electric vehicles.

The Volt had been a technological success, but it wasn't selling in big numbers. Neither was Nissan's Leaf. The Volt's best year would be 25,000 globally in 2012. Longtime GM engineers saw that as a pittance at a company that was used to selling 200,000 Chevy Impalas a year just in the US and four times as many large pickup trucks. They wanted to stick to the trucks, SUVs, and cars that made money.

"The existing product development organization had a lot of difficulty getting their arms around this," Girsky said. "Stevens didn't want to do it. So I had to go to Dan."

Internally, Girsky said, GM's engineers wanted to do everything themselves, including the battery. When GM developed the Volt, the company worked with LG but had its own battery lab where they tested different battery chemistry and the power storage units for durability. There were vaults that would subject batteries to extreme heat or cold temperatures. They had a table that would give the Volt's huge, T-shaped battery a boneshaker ride to simulate the toughest roads.

"The Bolt was a dogfight," Akerson said. "The Volt didn't sell that well. They said there weren't enough charging stations. But sometimes you gotta play ahead."

The way Akerson saw it, Henry Ford was working on mass production of cars when American roads were dirt paths with "stones, potholes, and horse shit." He wanted GM to get ahead of the game for a change and stop chasing the competition.

He sided with Girsky and put Barra, an electrical engineer, in a central role for the vehicle. He thought GM should work with LG. Better yet, he thought there should be a bake-off between GM's battery technology and LG's to see who could come up with the better power pack for GM's future EV, which would end up being the Chevy Bolt.

Akerson flew to Seoul to meet with LG Electronics. They had dinner at the chairman's house. It was Akerson, GM manufacturing head Tim Lee (an early mentor of Barra's), along with LG's top managers. Akerson said they were served a gutted pigeon with a hot stone in the center and put into a soup. It wasn't quite like the overdrawn scene from an Indiana Jones movie, but it was an awkward moment in the early stages of a relationship between GM and LG that would have highs and lows for years to come. He graciously and politely poked at the pigeon while Lee stuck to salad and whiskey.

"I said, 'I'll tell you what, if you can give us a better battery than we can do, there's nothing like competition and it can't be friendly,'" Akerson said. "I wanted an outside perspective. They won. They had better design and duration. I wanted the best battery pack for the customer. LG had better range, better cost. It was an easy decision."

By this time in 2011, Barra had replaced Stephens atop product development. Barra was more keen on the Bolt and getting GM into the electrification game. It was early days, but regulators were starting to push for cleaner cars across the globe, especially in China. GM also wanted to keep developing electric drive. The Bolt was a natural outgrowth of the Volt. It would show GM was moving to the next level.

Once the project was underway, the next debate was how much battery to put on board the Bolt, and it would be Barra's decision. In car making—especially new-tech cars like EVs that lost a lot of money—every dollar counts. So does every pound of weight. In 2012, when GM was starting the Bolt project, batteries were heavy, expensive, and didn't have near the power density of today's EVs. It was a tightrope walk to

strike the right balance of how much battery power to load
into the car, how much weight a bigger battery would add,
and how much the whole thing would cost.

This would be the moment when Barra really put her
stamp on the vehicle, and it presaged how she would lead GM
into electrification later on. The first version of the Bolt that
GM was developing behind the scenes could go between 100
and 150 miles on a full charge. Tesla's Elon Musk was promis-
ing well more than 200 miles for the Model S, which would
be a larger and faster luxury sedan. He also had the Model 3
in the works. GM hoped to beat him to market.

In a 2012 meeting, the Bolt team was discussing how
much battery to pack into the car and how much range to give
it. Girsky said Barra wasn't happy with 150 miles of range.
American consumers already saw electric cars as science projects that weren't practical for daily driving. Even worse, Tesla
would have the Model S for sale in 2012 with 265 miles of
range for its top-shelf version. GM would be hitting the market, albeit at a much lower sale price, with far less range.

If GM went out with less than 200 miles, the car would
be yesterday's news the day it went on sale. That's the kind of
decision making that got the company in trouble decades ago.
The Bolt was scheduled for sale in late 2016. By then, who
knew where Tesla's battery technology would be? Maybe Nissan's Leaf would leapfrog the Bolt, too.

Internally, some people didn't think it was worth putting
too much investment into plug-in cars. The biggest reason GM
made them was to meet clean-air requirements in California,
which is the largest vehicle market in the US.

Here's how the math worked in California at the time. GM
sold about 220,000 vehicles per model year in the state. To
avoid heavy fines or the threat of getting shut out of California
entirely, it would need state-awarded Zero-Emission Vehicle

(ZEV) credits equal to 14 percent of total sales. That's about 31,000, which would mean finding buyers for 7,700 Bolts, which earn four credits for each as an electric vehicle, or selling a little more than 10,000 Volt plug-in hybrids, or a combination of the two. Since both vehicles lost money, GM ideally wanted to sell enough to meet regulations and sell profitable trucks and SUVs, but not so many that it would pile on losses from the electrified models.

Since California is a big and lucrative market, carmakers engineered their green cars to meet minimal requirements. It wasn't until Tesla came along that anyone tried to make EVs something that consumers seriously craved. The Bolt wasn't exactly a looker, but Barra wanted the car to at least be competitive and show that GM had some technological chops.

"Mary challenged the team and said we have to get 200 miles or we're going to embarrass ourselves," Girsky said. "That was the first time I saw Mary assert herself in product development."

That was an important move for GM. For years, the company had put out small cars that were just good enough, or middle of the pack the day they went on sale. That meant that new models from competitors would quickly offer better features, a fresher look, and often newer technology within a year or two. That would leave GM's dealers to duke it out with competing models based on price instead of appeal.

Pushing the team to get at least 200 miles of range with a compact Bolt meant the car might not be a loser the day it was born. And they did it. When the Bolt went on sale in 2016, it could go more than 230 miles on a charge. Tesla's Model S could go at least 249, but was a larger car and typically sold for more than $100,000. The Bolt went for $42,000, but with a federal tax credit of $7,500, it became pretty affordable. Its range more than doubled Nissan's Leaf.

There were plenty of naysayers inside GM when it came to electric vehicles. Barra will listen to countervailing views on any strategy, Quattrone told me. But once a decision is made and a plan is set in motion, she won't tolerate complaining and sniping. She was particularly annoyed by CAVE people, the ones who are "Continually Against Virtually Everything."

"She would say, 'Get rid of the CAVE people,'" he told me. "Once we make a decision, don't walk out and say, 'This is a dumb idea.'"

Barra also had a polite way of telling people maybe GM is no longer the place for them. She sits on Disney's board of directors. In her own tough twist on the company's "Happiness is a state of mind" tagline, she had a polite way of finding an exit for people who wouldn't be part of the team.

"Mary is not soft," Quattrone said. "She used to say, 'If we have people who can't sign up for the strategy, go see John.' Or, 'If you don't like the plan, we will help you find happiness.'"

Her success with leaning up the organization and her politely tough style impressed Akerson. In 2013, his wife's cancer had gotten worse, and he was spending more and more of his time at home in Virginia with her. He hadn't moved to Detroit on a permanent basis, opting instead to buy an apartment at the Book Cadillac, a refurbished luxury hotel near headquarters. Girsky, whose residence was in New York, also lived there. The two would dine together frequently.

When Akerson was pondering an exit, he said he saw four people in a position to be considered to run the company. Mark Reuss, who was head of GM North America; Girsky; Ammann; and Barra. Before Akerson was in the CEO's job, Reuss had been a favorite to get the job next. Whitacre liked his passion for cars and thought he knew the nuts and bolts of the business better than anyone.

Akerson didn't think Reuss was ready. He did respect his engineering knowledge and said he is the heart and soul of the company, especially in product development. But he said he was too emotional. Barra promoted him later and told me that Reuss is passionate, not emotional, and the best car guy in the industry.

"When I got there, the sense was Mark Reuss would be the next CEO," Akerson said. "I eliminated him almost immediately. I told him I admired some of his skills but he didn't see a lot wrong with the company to look inside and lead them to a better place. I thought he needed more development."

Girsky was also a possibility, but only briefly. He had run GM's European operations and had gotten it closer to breaking even. But Akerson didn't think that he had the experience to be CEO of such a large organization.

"The problem is he has never been in a tough management position," Akerson said. "He had been a banker before. I didn't feel he had the experience."

Akerson decided he had two contenders to bring to the board, Barra and Ammann. Both had made big strides in the post-bankruptcy years. Barra had taken out a lot of workers, reduced costs, simplified management in product development, and started GM on the road to electric drive. The Bolt wasn't a huge seller. Compact cars never are. But it did get GM in the game at a time when only Nissan's Leaf and Tesla were selling pure electric cars in anything resembling sales volume. It was a technological achievement and had pushed the company's electrification program moving to the next step after the Volt.

Ammann had also impressed Akerson and the board. The former Morgan Stanley investment banker had worked on GM's bankruptcy and its initial public offering. After GM emerged, he took a job as the automaker's treasurer under CFO Chris Liddell. He eventually became CFO when Liddell quit, and Akerson also promoted Barra.

The tall, bearded New Zealander is quietly intense. He doesn't suffer fools and is known for being demanding with his staff. Though he came from the banking world, he has a passion for cars and driving and loved going to GM's proving ground in Milford, about forty-five miles outside Detroit, to tear it up on the test track.

He brought a fresh perspective to GM. He wondered, for example, why GM was doing business in so many places around the globe if the company lost money in many of those markets year in and year out. Ammann wanted better visibility into all of the company's markets.

Once Akerson had brought GM's IT in house, the company had better control of its own data and information. Ammann upgraded GM's systems to track how much every model made or lost in every market in the world. With better information, the company could decide what to keep, what to dump, and what models needed work to improve profits. His work would be a key piece as the company restructured its overseas operations later on.

He and Akerson took a hard look at GM's European operations. The company was building inexpensive cars in Korea and shipping them to Europe to sell under the Chevy name. The small cars were sold in existing Opel dealerships at a 10 percent discount to the German brand's Astra compact.

GM was keeping excess production in Korea to serve Europe rather than making the hard choice of closing plants. Then the company sold those cheap cars in Europe and undermined the value of the Opel cars that were for sale on the same showroom floor. Opel's brand image was already cut-rate compared to Volkswagen and sold for lower prices than

BARRA'S RISE

Ford. Selling cheap Chevy cars on the same floor put even more downward pressure on pricing.

Akerson had a meeting with the team. He was apoplectic about the Korea-to-Europe connection. He pretended to hit his head on the table and asked, "Do you guys do this because you like to get headaches? You guys are destroying brand value here and overproducing there."

In December 2013, GM stopped selling Chevy in Europe, and in the years after, restructured in Korea. The company would close a plant in Gunsan several years later. That would just be the beginning of its global restructuring.

Barra and Ammann had both shown a willingness to be decisive, look at the company's warts, and push people out of their comfort zones. Akerson thought they could bring change.

According to three people who were involved in the process, lead director Patricia Russo had briefly put her name forward to lead the company since both Barra and Ammann had only been in their C-suite jobs for three years. But that didn't get very far. There was also an idea floated to make Girsky non-executive chairman to look over the shoulder of the new CEO, but that, too, was quickly dismissed.

Early on, both candidates had their supporters. Tim Solso, the retired CEO of semi-truck engine maker Cummins Inc., pushed for Barra with female directors Carol Stephenson and Kathy Marinello supporting her. Some of the male directors favored Ammann.

Akerson thought both were great candidates. So he had each one come up with a plan for how they would run the company, what their strategic priorities would be, and what they would change.

"I told Dan and Mary, 'It's you two. Give me your image for the company,'" Akerson said. "They each did, and they were a little different, not significantly. I brought them together and had them look at their plans. I said, "Would you stay if Mary gets picked and she follows her plan; would you stay? You'd be president."

Ammann took a day to think about it. He came back to Akerson and said he would stay on as president under Barra, who told Akerson she would serve under Ammann if he won the job. The two of them told the entire board, the same thing.

"They said, 'We want to tell you, the board, we are willing to take either of the two roles and if you pick one as leader and the other as president, we will work for each other,'" Isdell said. "Sitting on the board and hearing that was really quite remarkable. The right choice was Mary, but there was good discussion. Ammann didn't have empathetic leadership. Very smart man but didn't have those qualities that very clearly Mary had."

At the December 2013 board meeting, the directors voted unanimously to make Barra the CEO, with Ammann as president and chief operating officer. The auto industry's glass ceiling had been completely shattered. Barra would be its first female CEO. Solso became non-executive chairman and Reuss became head of product development.

CHAPTER 5

⚡

IGNITION SWITCH FIASCO

Barra's time in the limelight went sour quickly. Soon after she took over, GM would go through one of the most shameful and tortured events in its history, which is saying something for a company that went from most respected in the world to bankrupt. An ignition switch on several of GM's cheapest models had a fatal flaw that company engineers, attorneys, and managers had either been trying to ignore, wish away, or—in the case of the engineer who designed it—cover up for years. Despite their best and worst efforts, that switch would be yanked into the public domain on her watch. The very integrity of GM and Barra herself would face even tougher scrutiny than the automaker did when Wagoner had gone to Washington seeking a bailout.

The whole episode started coming to the surface tragically in March 2010, while Barra was most likely negotiating executive compensation with Treasury Department pay czar Kenneth Feinberg or handling such weighty matters as the simplification of GM's starchy dress code. About 800 miles away, twenty-nine-year-old pediatric nurse Brooke Melton was driving her white 2005 Chevy Cobalt on Highway 9 in

Georgia when the ignition switch shut off. Melton lost control of the car and veered into the southbound lane, where she hit another car. The impact with that vehicle sent her Cobalt off the road, down an embankment, and into a creek. She died from injuries sustained in the crash.

Her father was dumfounded by the accident because there was no apparent cause for his daughter to have just lost control of the car. While going through Brooke's mail he found a recall notice for the car's power steering system. Convinced that was the problem, he contacted attorney Lance Cooper to talk about a wrongful death suit. Cooper said it sounded plausible and took the case. To get a handle on the problem, Cooper hired mechanic Charlie Miller, who ran a repair shop in Merigold, Mississippi, and served as an expert witness in auto crash cases, to look at Brooke's car and sleuth out the cause of the accident.

Miller may have been a small-town mechanic, but he was no Goober Pyle. After inspecting the car, he told Cooper that his case had a problem; it wasn't the power steering. He unearthed the mangled car's black box, which told him that the vehicle had just shut down. The box said the car went from fifty-eight miles per hour to zero in an instant. The car didn't stop that fast, of course. That was Miller's clue that the ignition had simply shut off. Miller then dug into GM's warranty and service letters to customers and discovered that, in 2005, GM had issued a service bulletin saying that the car could shut off while driving due to the switch's low torque rating. With minimal force, the switch could slip out of "run" and into the "accessory" position, which shuts off the engine, airbags, and power steering and brakes. If it happened, the car would have no power and the driver would be stripped bare of the protections typically afforded by airbags. They were completely exposed if there was an accident.

Cooper said he was starting to unearth a cover-up. GM issued a service bulletin rather than a recall, which would enable the company to avoid the cost of repairing every compact car on the road. And to make sure GM didn't have to recall anything, the company used the term "shut off" rather than "stalled" in the bulletin, Cooper said, because "stalling" tips off the National Highway Traffic and Safety Administration that a recall would need to be done. Recalls can be very expensive.

Cooper filed an amended lawsuit in 2013 on behalf of Brooke Melton's parents saying that the company designed a poor ignition switch. He then got a judge in Cobb County, Georgia, to force GM to hand over documents related to the switch. That's when the land mines started going off. Cooper discovered a few facts that would affirm the worst things that people thought about GM and its reputed savings-first, customer-second culture. The documents showed that the company knew there were problems with the switch ten years earlier. The cost to give the switch a better spring that would have solved the problem was fifty-seven cents a car. Cobalt program director Gary Altman said in 2004 that replacing the switches "was not an acceptable business decision," according to court documents. It also came out that GM had ordered parts maker Delphi to make the original switch in a way that didn't meet the automaker's own requirements for how much torque was required to turn the car on and off. It required too little torque to move it.

The more Cooper found, the worse things got for GM. He hired an engineer named Mark Hood to inspect the switch. He bought a new replacement switch and compared it to an older model. He noticed that the pin and spring that create the torque were different in the new switch he bought from the one in Melton's car. That indicated that GM had actually fixed the switch—thus acknowledging a problem—without telling anyone. When GM's outside attorney saw that, he called it a "bombshell," Cooper said.

The case finally had serious attention from GM attorneys in Detroit in 2013. But it wouldn't hit Barra until January. She got a call from Mark Reuss as she was headed home from work saying the ignition problem was going to need a recall and it could be a big one.[1] It started out at nearly 800,000 cars, which is big but not completely unusual in the auto business. By the next month it had doubled. Meanwhile, Cooper and other attorneys were finding more clients. Media coverage was also compounding. As reporters started poring over the documents obtained by Cooper, it was becoming clear that GM had buried the switch problem internally for years.

Massive recalls like this are a nightmare for any CEO. It would be even tougher for Barra, who at that point was not the kind of executive who enjoyed the spotlight. Quite the opposite. To this day, she would rather credit the team than herself, is fiercely private, and always carries herself in a very composed state of dignity and professionalism. The press-shy CEO was then summoned to go before Congress and the Senate in early April. At that point, GM didn't know how many people were killed or injured by the switch. Eventually, 124 deaths and many more injuries were linked to the switch, but GM had confirmed only a fraction of that when Barra headed to Washington.

Barra had little chance of escaping the hearing with anything but a public stoning. That's just how Washington is. The hearings are held with the pretense of finding information, but the real purpose is penance on prime-time TV. For a CEO under fire, there are only degrees of losing. For politicians, it's a risk-free way to make a stand against big companies without angering people in any corner of the electorate. Take on GM with tougher fuel economy rules and union leaders will complain about job losses. Vote in favor of a bailout and Republicans will call it socialism. Vote against it and union leaders and Democrats will say they are presiding over job loss. But beat up a CEO over a faulty product? Voters of any persuasion are pretty OK with that.

Internally, GM's general counsel Mike Millikin and Barra had already decided that they needed a full and thorough investigation of what happened before they could explain anything to Congress, but they hadn't had time to get it done. To spearhead the internal probe, they reached out to Chicago attorney Anton Valukas, who had been appointed by a court to investigate the 2009 bankruptcy of investment bank Lehman Bros. He concluded that the investment bank not only misread the growing risks in the mortgage business, but had also manipulated its books using accounting trickery to hide them from the market. That report had given him credibility as an honest broker, even if he was a corporate-side attorney.

Barra wanted to hire him and give him free rein to do a "full and open investigation" into what happened and who knew what and when. Valukas told me that Millikin had called him at Barra's behest before the April 1 congressional hearing. He wouldn't be able to get enough work done to help Barra when she went to Washington.

"What I remember is her saying, 'We are going to scour these records to ensure we don't have other issues that raise safety concerns and we're going to get it all done at once,'" Valukas said. "All the cards are going faceup on the table. She was insistent."

Millikin was also in favor of hiring Kenneth Feinberg to help oversee a fund for victims, but he didn't want to say too much about it in Washington. Nor did he want to make promises about victim compensation before GM had a handle on potential costs, said people familiar with the conversations. The Feinberg fund was central to Barra's strategy to take care of GM's customers and the victims and restore the company's reputation. Thanks to bankruptcy, the company had a legal mechanism to stiff-arm legal claims. Bankruptcy law gave GM a shield against litigation for any products or defects that occurred prior to the 2009 Chapter 11 filing. Barra knew GM couldn't hide behind the bankruptcy shield. Victims' families would be livid, and GM's reputation would be in tatters. But she also didn't have time to hash out how it would work before she got to Washington. So the plan was to stay quiet on details.

In early March, she called Cadillac president Bob Ferguson for advice. Ferguson had been given that job by Akerson, even though a lot of his experience had been in government affairs for AT&T. He was down in Miami at the Doral Open golf tournament, where Caddy sponsored the event. He told her she should tell Congress about Valukas and Feinberg and explain how the company was going to come clean and take care of victims. Ferguson thought he had her convinced, but before the hearing Millikin pulled back, and Barra went in with the story that old GM created the switch and new GM would try to figure out what happened.

Members of Congress and the Senate didn't care. Even before the hearing started, victims and lawmakers gathered outside and held a press conference. Senators Richard Blumenthal of Connecticut and Ed Markey of Massachusetts laid into GM.[2]

"GM's failure to act in the face of additional death, injuries, and complaints went on and on until just two months ago," Markey railed. "This recall is a decade late and dozens of lives and injuries short."

Blumenthal held up the photo of crash victim and Marine veteran Richard Scott Bailey in his dress blues. He then accused GM of hiding the defect to push its discovery past the bankruptcy. That would enable GM to use the bankruptcy shield to avoid big settlements.

"GM made a business decision to hide a defect, not only to avoid repairing it but to conceal it," Blumenthal said. "It concealed it not only from customers and employees, it concealed it from the United States government and thereby game the system to obtain a complete shield, broad and blanket immunity from liability from the lethal defects that it concealed."

Once the hearings started, Barra was in a shooting gallery facing both parties. Colorado Democrat Diana DeGette held up the ignition assembly and showed how easily the key could slip out of the start position, especially if the driver had a heavy key ring. She took a subtle shot that must have been biting to Barra since both of them have children.

"If you had a heavy keychain, like my mom's keychain, or if you were short and bumped up against the ignition with your knee, it could cause the ignition to switch right off," DeGette said.

DeGette and Pennsylvania Republican Tim Murphy wanted to know why GM didn't replace the switch a decade ago. They also pressed her on why the company would have risked driver safety for fifty-seven cents. Barra didn't have answers.

That number was the most damning fact of the entire case. It was just the kind of penny pinching for which GM was notorious. And it's the kind of thing that makes the public cynical about big corporations. It gave rise to the nastiest question about GM. This was the company we spent $11 billion to save? The one that wouldn't spend fifty-seven cents to ensure the safety of its customers and then covered it up for a decade?

The next day, Barra and her staff were walking into the Senate hearing when they ran into Missouri democrat Claire McCaskill, who was chair of the proceedings. They had a friendly conversation, but it ended with a surprising disclosure from McCaskill—one that shows just what a kabuki dance these hearings are. "I'm going to play to the cameras here and this is going to be awful for you," she said, according to a person who witnessed the conversation. "But this is what we do in Washington. Don't take it personally."

And play to the cameras she did. McCaskill told Barra that GM had a "culture of cover-up." She also went after Barra for not having fired anyone at that point, particularly Ray DeGiorgio, the engineer who had designed the switch and later surreptitiously changed the part without revealing that there had been a problem. He had even lied in depositions about making the change, Cooper said. McCaskill may have been going full vaudeville, but had a legitimate criticism when she said, "I can't understand for the life of me why he still has a job."

Nevada republican Dean Heller wanted to know what GM knew when the Treasury Department was giving GM $50 billion and all but accused the company of fraud. "It looks like GM was not forthcoming with the American people who bailed them out," said Heller.

Barbara Boxer of California laid into Barra personally for providing little clarity and accused her of being the very kind of old GM executive that she was supposed to have replaced. "You don't know anything about anything," Boxer said. "If this is the new GM leadership, it's pretty lacking. Woman to woman, I am very disappointed," Boxer said, "because the culture you're representing here is the culture of the status quo."

Barra remained stoic. She wasn't drawn in by any of the personal jabs, but she didn't look like she had things under control, either. She often wore a pained look on her face. She did announce that she had brought Feinberg on to set up a fund for victims, but with no detail on who would be covered or how much cash would be made available. As for answers, the best she could do was say that GM was looking into what the company knew and that she would take "appropriate action" when the company had reached conclusions.

"I cannot tell you why it took years for a safety defect to be announced," Barra told a House Energy and Commerce Committee investigative panel. "I can tell you that we will find out."

Days later, she was lampooned on *Saturday Night Live* with Kate McKinnon brilliantly cast and playing a Barra that just wanted to slink out of the room. As embarrassing as that was, the next months would be a lot tougher.

As coverage of the case hit maximum volume, reporters scoured legal documents that revealed the attempt by managers and engineers to cover it up. DeGiorgio had found problems with the part years earlier. He even ordered up changes in 2006 to include a stronger spring and plunger that added torque, making it more difficult for the ignition to slip out of drive. In an internal memo, DeGiorgio called it "the switch from hell." To save face, he didn't give the new version of the switch a part number. He kept the old part number. In so doing, GM's own internal investigators didn't know that a change had been made to fix a problem. That not only helped avoid issuing a public recall of the cars, but it would throw off GM's investigators for years, Cooper said.

Valukas went to work interviewing everyone involved in the switch, including Barra herself and other top executives. He said Barra told him that everyone at GM works in a silo. They rarely know what's going on in other areas of the company, so if there are problems it can be hard to find the information.

"It wasn't that they were bad people doing bad things," he recalls. "They were people doing things in their silo and had no idea what people in another silo were doing."

One of the most stunning revelations was that GM engineers saw a vehicle that would shut off while driving as a "convenience issue." They figured if the switch turned off while driving, the driver could just restart it quickly. It's a mere inconvenience! They also didn't understand how deadly that was. GM engineers didn't realize that the ignition switch in "accessory" would disable airbags, the Valukas report said.

It is a shocking discovery that engineers would view a car that shuts off while being driven as a mere inconvenience, not a highway hazard. It's also disturbing that they didn't view the problem as an embarrassment to GM's ability to make a quality car.

There was plenty of other corporate foolery that set GM up for this mess. The company's own internal cost policies provided a disincentive to issue a recall even if it was discovered in the early days of a car going on sale. If the Cobalt team wanted to issue a recall for a part, that meant other cars with the switch, like the Saturn Ion and Pontiac G5, had to do it. But the Cobalt team had to pay for those, too. So it would hurt the profitability—or in the cases of some of these models, add to its losses—and make the team look bad, Valukas's report said.

Barra herself gave Valukas a description of why things didn't get done at GM. People would meet, agree on a course of action, and then nothing would happen. "The GM nod, Barra described, is when everyone nods in agreement to a proposed plan of action, but then leaves the room with no intention of following through." There was also the GM salute, when employees would cross their arms and point outward, with the idea being that the problem was everyone else's responsibility.

While GM was nodding, saluting, and trying to ignore or cover up the ignition defect, accidents were happening, and people were dying. Outsiders were also discovering the problem. In 2005, a *New York Times* review of the Cobalt revealed the issue. After the *Times* called GM about it, one of the company's safety attorneys asked engineers if there was a problem, but did not ask if there was any risk to customers. He was trying to marshal evidence that the ignition shut off was inconsequential, Valukas discovered. The report also said that GM investigated the switch in 2005 but opened and closed the case in a month without doing anything. A young engineer found numerous customer complaints about the switch but the committee in charge of safety investigations did nothing. Company investigators had also looked for causes for why some airbags in the car didn't deploy, but they didn't find the cause even though they had information in their own files that would have pointed them in the right direction, the report said. In fact, a Wisconsin state trooper made the connection in April 2007. So did a research team from Indiana University. GM had a copy of the Wisconsin trooper's report but did nothing with it.

Here's where DeGiorgio's malfeasance really did damage. GM's internal investigators had a tough time understanding the problem because the car stopped shutting off with the 2008 model year. That's the first year that the new switch was put into the car, but GM investigators didn't know it because DeGiorgio didn't change the part number. Internally, GM thought the exact same switch stopped involuntarily shutting off, the report said.

The case didn't reach the vice president level at GM until December 17, 2013. That's when internal investigators presented their findings to the Executive Field Action Decision Committee, the star chamber that decides on recalls.

The top-ranking execs were Chief Engineer John Calabrese, Quality Senior Vice President Alicia Boler Davis, and head of manufacturing Gerald Johnson. Valukas said Johnson didn't attend. Boler Davis sent a proxy and Calabrese said he wanted more data before issuing a recall. Calabrese brought the issue to Barra's attention at that time. She told him, "Get the right data; do the right thing."

In another damning look at the slow pace of GM's bureaucracy, the EFADC didn't meet again until January 31, 2014. Boler Davis showed up in person with Calabrese and a group of GM attorneys. At that meeting, the team presented evidence and cause that the switch should shut off if a driver's knee hit the keychain or in rough driving conditions. Since their report was compiled in 2011, they didn't have the most current data on the problem and voted to recall just 780,000 vehicles. The recall quickly grew to 2.6 million vehicles as Barra and Reuss sought to get every one of the switches fixed.

Valukas's report came out on May 29. Barra digested it and began planning what to do next. Publicly, she described the Valukas findings as "extremely thorough, brutally tough, and deeply troubling." In a prepared statement, she went on to say, "Overall the report found that, from start to finish, the Cobalt saga was riddled with failures which led to tragic results for many," while noting that the report revealed no conspiracy by the company to cover up the facts and no evidence that any employee made a trade-off between safety and cost. It may not have been a widespread conspiracy, but at least DeGiorgio had tried to conceal it years earlier. What the report concluded was that upper management was never notified of the problem, and consequently couldn't have conspired to hide it from regulators. It also said that the problem was caused by ineptitude and not skullduggery.

GM's top executives going all the way to Akerson had no idea what was coming. Carmakers get sued all the time. Years later, Cooper told me that he found no evidence that the switch problems ever got to the upper levels of management, including to CEO Akerson or Barra, who was running product development and purchasing at the time of the lawsuit.

Akerson told me that he was interviewed by the Justice Department about what he knew. He said they had thousands of internal GM emails about the switch.

"Did you see one with my name on it?" he asked the attorneys. "They hadn't," he said.

Valukas's findings depicted a deadly version of the movie *Office Space*, with weak controls, slow-moving committees, and company silos bumbling around and all but ensuring that nothing was done. Barra released it to the public so that everyone could see all of GM's warts. It exposed the company's cultural problems for all to see. Everyone could read about the bad engineering, the inept internal investigations, the committees that met and did nothing, engineers covering their asses, the GM nod, and the GM salute. It had all of the bad behavior that people associated with big corporations like GM.

For years, GM dismissed media reports about its culture as the product of hacks who wouldn't give the company a fair shake. This time, the blame was plastered all over multiple levels of the company. Barra said it was a gut punch. Even though she had identified bad GM management practices in her presentation for Harry Pearce's presentation fourteen years earlier and told Valukas that she used to call people out for giving the GM nod, she found the revelations to be a tough read.

"The day I read [the Valukas report] was one of the saddest days of my career," Barra told *Time*.[3] "The most frightening part to me was that the report said everything that everyone's criticized us about."

It was also, at long last, an honest assessment of where GM really was in its cultural transformation. GM was nowhere. There was a hope that bankruptcy and the years of a no-BS boss like Akerson would have changed the culture, lit a fire under GM. Yet there GM was four years after emerging from Chapter 11 and insiders were just starting to raise a flag about the switch even as evidence was mounting that it was a problem. Even though those cars were still on the road.

To her credit, Barra didn't have to publish the whole report but did anyway, Valukas said. She could have just released a summary. It was legally risky. By handing out the entire thing, Barra was drawing a battle plan for plaintiffs' lawyers, the state attorneys general, and the Department of Justice, and giving all of them ordinance. All would have a blueprint to extract money and settlements from GM and levy massive fines. Valukas said that Barra didn't express concern over any of that.

"What she authorized us to do was extraordinary. She told us that we were going to make full disclosures to the US Attorney's office," Valukas said. "There was nothing that said she had to do all the things she did."

Then she rolled some heads, firing fifteen executives and punishing five more. The company didn't release specifics, but names got out. DeGiorgio was canned. The highest-ranking employee was Mike Robinson, who was GM's vice president of sustainability and global regulatory affairs. He allegedly had urged an employee who Barra fired, safety director Gay Kent, to push back against NHTSA claims that GM responds slowly to recalls. Safety attorney Bill Kemp was also let go as was Carmen Benavides, who was head of safety investigations, according to Bloomberg.[4]

Barra's next move was to address the whole of GM and make it clear that what happened could never occur again. She stood, in a plain blue suit coat and white shirt, at a podium before a crowded auditorium at GM's engineering center in Warren, Michigan, and had the speech broadcast to GM's global offices and the media. The message was clear: GM needed to change its behavior.

"For those of us who have dedicated our lives to this company, it is enormously painful to see our shortcomings laid out so vividly," she said. "As I read this report I was deeply disturbed. I want it known that this recall is not just an engineering or a recall problem. With these vehicles we simply didn't do our jobs. We will use this as a template to strengthen our company. Repeatedly, individuals failed to disclose fundamental pieces of information that could have fundamentally changed the lives of those impacted by the faulty ignition switch. If this information had been disclosed this company would have dealt with it differently."

Her message also came with a warning. "If you are aware of a potential problem affecting safety or quality and you don't speak up, then you are part of the problem," Barra said.

The Valukas report was well received in media coverage. And against the backdrop of a company that had traditionally fought every ounce of criticism, it seemed self-effacing and tough. But not everyone was impressed. Blumenthal put out a release criticizing the report because Valukas was paid by GM. He called it "the best report money can buy. It absolves upper management, denies deliberate wrongdoing, and dismisses corporate culpability."

Cooper also criticized it. He said it was tough enough to make GM look like it was owning up to its sins. But he had communications saying that the GM general counsel's office knew about the case years before and had covered it up. He thought the move was smart by Barra, but stopped short of saying that certain employees, especially GM's attorneys, tried to cover up the problem.

"They said Valukas didn't pull any punches and portrayed GM in a bad light, but he didn't go too far. That was Barra's purpose," he said in an interview. "There were letters going back to 2006 where there was a cover-up with the general counsel's office. That was one of my biggest problems is that the lawyers absolutely participated in the cover-up."

Barra moved to set up an early warning program. Solso, the non-executive chairman, was appalled at GM's process for elevating defects to upper management and helped Barra craft a new one. "When I was at Cummins, if we had a sniff of a product problem, I knew within twenty-four hours," he said. "GM had all these committees. They didn't keep minutes from the meetings because the lawyers wouldn't let them."

Barra launched an internal program called "Speak Up for Safety" that rewarded employees for identifying potential quality issues early. When an intern flagged an overheating fuel pump in his family's Cadillac, GM was able to find the problem, recall just 10,000 cars, and fix the part for future production. That headed off a much wider recall. Barra took the intern to lunch. The company also hired staff to monitor social media, chat rooms, and dealer complaints for issues, rather than waiting on NHTSA to flag problems. Ammann said top executives even worked the phone lines and chat rooms.

"We will get past this, but we can't forget the most important thing we've learned," he told me at the time.[5]

The Feinberg fund was Barra's most savvy move. She knew Feinberg from his days as the Treasury Department's paymaster for companies that took a bailout. Barra told him that GM would set up the parameters of who gets paid, but after that the company and its lawyers would walk away and let him do the job.

"Mary, if somebody is a drunk driver or speeding or driving without a license or was contributorily negligent so their fault contributed to the accident, should those be reasons why GM doesn't pay?" Feinberg asked. She said, "You're right. Contributory negligence. We'll pay regardless of contributing circumstances."

There was no cap on the size of the fund, but there were some limits. The idea, Feinberg said, was to pay out claims to make sure no one who was a true victim felt GM had hid from its responsibilities. Claimants had to prove that the ignition switch failed. The car's black box could show it. Failure of the power steering and brakes or airbags did, too. As long as that was the case, GM would pay, he said. GM even paid settlements in unsympathetic cases. Feinberg said he had one claim in which three teenagers died in an accident when police were chasing them at ninety miles an hour. The ignition shut off and they lost control.

Cooper was quick to point out that the fund wasn't pure altruism. Feinberg settled the riskiest cases, but without paying punitive damages. The fund paid pain and suffering, which was capped at a certain level, plus lost wages. That kept payouts at a manageable level, Cooper said, adding that in a few cases where he refused Feinberg's money, he was able to sue and get more than the fund was paying on average.

Of the 4,343 claims against GM, Feinberg paid out 399 of them, or 9 percent, for a total of $590 million. Most of the ineligible claims involved a vehicle that either didn't have the defective switch or that was hit by someone else and the safety equipment worked, Feinberg said. Still, the death total climbed to 124, which was far more than GM had estimated earlier.

Barra met some of the families. In April, after the first hearings in Washington, Texas plaintiffs' attorney Bob Hilliard set up a meeting with Barra and her staff to meet families of the victims. There were at least a dozen there. She treated them with respect and repeatedly said, "I'm sorry for your loss," one of the people who attended the meetings said. People in the meeting said Barra appeared deeply moved.

By June it was clear that Barra was getting a handle on the public damage. That month, McCaskill had a second hearing. This time she was complimentary of Barra but had it in for Millikin and the general counsel for GM's North America business, Lucy Clark Dougherty. It was Dougherty's job to keep Millikin abreast of legal claims. McCaskill charged that, at minimum, Dougherty and Millikin were incompetent because there were civil suits and other claims about the ignition switch right under their noses and they never noticed or did anything about them.

"The culture of lawyering up to minimize liability killed innocent customers of General Motors," McCaskill said. "I'm even more interested today in understanding the aftermath of this report, how in the world did Michael Millikin keep his job? I do not understand how did the general counsel for a litigation department that had this massive failure of responsibility, how he would be allowed to continue to keep an important leadership role in this company."

When Millikin had a chance to defend himself, he claimed attorneys reporting to him and Dougherty had kept them in the dark. Those same lawyers were among the fifteen executives who were fired, Barra said in her general counsel's defense. While McCaskill made it clear that she approved of

IGNITION SWITCH FIASCO

Barra's handling of the crisis, she thought more people needed to be fired.

"So I don't get how you and Lucy Clark Dougherty still have your jobs," she said. "Ms. Barra, can you explain that to me?"

Barra defended Millikin and said she needed someone with his integrity and experience. But it was a fair question. Millikin was the general counsel, whose job is to safeguard GM and its shareholders from legal risk. He had a moral obligation to protect the company's customers and employees. His department failed those missions and there he was, still employed.

In fact, only one vice president had been fired among the fifteen executives. No other top executives lost their jobs. McCaskill let it go. Barra was starting to look the part of a CEO who was in control.

"I think you've done a lot of good work since you took over," McCaskill said. "I think you've handled this with courage and conviction."

The Justice Department felt the same way. In September 2015, the Feds fined GM $900 million. Preet Bharara, the US Attorney for New York's Southern District, said that GM's disclosures during the investigation played a role in the relatively small fine. Not only did Barra and Valukas reveal the company's failings, but GM's internal investigators kept turning over more information as the probe went on.

"Good behavior after the fact does not absolve GM or any company of responsibility," Bharara said during the press conference. "But companies should be encouraged to act as GM did here to help the truth come out faster."

That's much different than the treatment Toyota got a year earlier when the Japanese automaker was fined $1.2 billion after recalling more than 9 million vehicles several years earlier for accelerator problems. That was the largest fine for an automaker in history. Toyota was hit harder because the Justice Department found internal documents saying there were problems with the company's vehicles, while its public communication downplayed any risk to drivers. US attorney general Eric Holder called the company's behavior "shameful."

Investors were starting to notice Barra's deft handling of the case. During the crisis, Warren Buffett told CNN, "She's dynamite. You couldn't have a better CEO," just before he loaded up on the stock.

CHAPTER 6

⚡

BARRA IN CHARGE

By the start of 2015, Barra was getting a firm handle on the ignition crisis. After a year of toiling with the sins of old GM, she could finally start to set her agenda for a new GM. She needed to scrutinize where GM was spending its money and start setting priorities. At this point, she knew the company couldn't continue to fund every vehicle and play in every market that it had traditionally supported. Not with Silicon Valley giants like Google and Apple and cheeky upstarts like Uber and Tesla seeking to upend transportation. She needed to quickly figure out how GM would handle new technology like electric vehicles, self-driving software, and trends like ridesharing. If she played it right, GM could be a contender or even a leader and she would transform the company. If she made the wrong choices, GM would fade once again and there might not be another second chance from the US government or from American consumers.

GM had already been scrutinizing its global operations. Bankruptcy had restructured the US business, and the company made cuts in Canada. But it hadn't really fixed the overseas businesses. Whitacre and Akerson had both been looking at them and Barra was part of a management team that was asking tough questions about those operations. With Akerson's unplanned departure (his wife's health had worsened) it was up to Barra to decide whether GM would continue to be the global empire that was always, at some point, touched by daylight, or if the company should lean down to a smaller, more profitable core.

At a budget meeting in GM's headquarters early that year, the international team was asking for $1 billion to fund new models for markets in Southeast Asia, namely Indonesia and Thailand. Barra and then-CFO Chuck Stevens were pushing the team on why it was a smart investment. They said that GM had to spend the money to stay relevant in those markets.

"We have to do this," she recalls being told. "I said, 'We don't have to do anything.'"[1]

That conversation would frame Barra's strategy as she set about dismantling global operations in what would be the biggest strategic change for the company since Alfred Sloan started expanding abroad by first acquiring Germany's Opel AG in 1929 and Holden of Australia two years after that. She and Ammann were already taking an almost callous look at what businesses GM should keep and what it should dump. They knew that GM couldn't continue to pour money into so many far-flung locales.

It wasn't arbitrary. The company stayed in so many markets because the company had been the largest in the world for decades. GM had been number one until 2009. And even then, it was in a dogfight with Toyota and Volkswagen for top ranking in global vehicle sales. Retreating from a market, even one that lost money, seemed like losing on purpose. But Barra knew she would have to cut back in these places if the company were to gain respect with investors and if she were ever to be able to afford to compete with her longstanding rivals and new threats from Silicon Valley.

"We had managing directors asking for money dedicated to product programs that weren't going to be profitable in a region that wasn't going to be profitable," Barra told me. "If we don't have a plan, we just can't deploy money. There was a mindset that said, 'we have to.'"

She was going to overhaul all of it. If a region or product line didn't have a chance at making fat returns, it would be on the block. They had to. Investors were growing bored with the tepid returns of established car companies. They were becoming increasingly fixated on Big Tech and Tesla. The only way Barra could invest in new technology was if she diverted capital from dying portions of GM's old business and into the new one.

There were real threats on the horizon. Silicon Valley companies were looking at the $3 trillion in annual revenue that carmakers fight over, and figuring that they could get a piece of it. They not only had the attention of investors, but those companies also had a hold on the kind of affluent, coastal consumers that GM coveted. Tesla, Google, and Uber could not be ignored. All three presented a fresh alternative to the hoary business of selling cars to people who wanted to drive their own gasoline-burning vehicle around every day. Uber's ride hailing service was really catching on, especially in big cities. Rather than running to a corner and shouting and waving for a cab or parking in some pricey garage, people were tapping an app on their phone and getting a driver to come to them. Sales were quadrupling and Uber would finish 2015 at nearly $2 billion. Yellow Cab was being upended and Uber became a verb in the same way that Xerox had become synonymous with making copies decades before and Google had become a verb for web search. If more people wanted to buy transportation by the ride instead of at the dealership, GM and the established car companies were in trouble.

Tesla was not going bankrupt the way so many industry insiders and short sellers had predicted and hoped. Sales of the Model S were growing and would reach almost 19,000 in 2015. That may be tiny to a company like GM, which sold more than 9 million cars and trucks a year. But the electric Model S was a technological tour de force that could go more than 260 miles on a charge and upgrade driving performance with over-the-air software changes. Musk and the Tesla brand were achieving cult-like status and he proved luxury buyers would embrace electric drive.

So were investors. Girsky's "Team Tesla" had been monitoring the company's technological developments and its growth as a business for several years. A master at fund raising, Musk at that point had raised $5 billion from stock and convertible debt. He also had borrowed $465 million from the federal government under the Obama administration, but used other funds he raised to pay it back. The company was getting ready to sell the Model X, a midsized SUV that took square aim at the heart of the luxury market, and the smaller, cheaper Model 3. If Detroit companies were in denial that Tesla would survive, they were mistaken. Musk's new models were selling out and investors were snapping up his stock and debt. Despite piling up losses, Tesla's market value far exceeded Fiat Chrysler's and it was inching closer to the value of GM and Ford.

The other thing GM was watching was Google's development of self-driving software. The company had shown off its two-seat, egg-shaped self-driving car the year before, right about the time Barra was reading the Valukas report. It was quirky. The little pod had two bug eyes, a black puppy nose, and only went twenty-five miles per hour. But it did so without a human controlling the pedals and wheel. GM also had an autonomous vehicle program, but Google had been working on it longer and was ahead of all comers when it came to robotic drive. While GM's car was having trouble swerving around parked cars, Google was getting a robot ready to get its driving permit.

While GM was chasing Tesla and Google in technology development, Barra had a cash disadvantage. She didn't have Google's $73 billion, which was the search giant's cash hoard at the time. She also couldn't dedicate $5 billion just for electric cars the way Musk did. In fact, at the time, Barra had been tussling with a group of activist investors led by hedge fund Appaloosa Management and Harry Wilson, a former Treasury Department official who had a big role in the restructuring of GM during the financial crisis. After months of pressure and negotiating, Barra agreed to $5 billion in share buybacks. She also agreed that GM would keep a cash cushion of $20 billion and use the rest to invest in the business and buy more stock if they had cash. She bought $5 billion in 2015 and another $5 billion in shares after that. GM also paid out $2.2 billion a year in dividends. Neither Tesla nor Google paid a dividend.

But hey, that's the tough break when investors view a company like GM as a cyclical dividend payer and not a growth stock. In the looming tech war, it was a serious disadvantage. Musk had investors lining up to give him capital. Google was throwing off more than $16 billion a year in free cash flow, and amping that up every year. Barra was getting out of a crisis and, despite strong profits at GM, was still trying to impress Wall Street.

"We ran into ignition switch, then you pop out the other side of that and you have all this potential change," Dan Ammann said in an interview. "Electrification, self-driving, and so on. The general realization in the middle of 2015 was that there was a lot of change afoot. I don't think anyone realized how big it would be or how expensive it would be or how soon it would be, just kind of a sense that if we ignore all of these things it's to our own peril. That led to the impetus for a more ruthless evaluation of the existing portfolio."

Barra had to take out the axe. In reality, the company made almost all of its profits in the US and China. In 2014, GM's pretax profit in North America was $6.6 billion. If not for recall costs, which shouldn't be ignored, GM would have made $9 billion. The China business made $2.1 billion in pretax profits. GM lost $1.4 billion in Europe and $200 million in South America. The rest of the company's GM International Operations unit lost about $800 million. In other words, if you take away China profits, GM's overseas businesses lost $2.5 billion. That was a pretty typical performance from the global enterprise outside the US and China.

When Ammann was CFO, he had installed controls to track GM's profits and losses around the globe. That way GM could see how much work they would need to do to boost fortunes in dozens of markets where the company sold vehicles. Whitacre and Akerson had also been eyeing up the problems. Pearce said Barra had discussed GM's outsized structure with him years earlier.

"Part of Mary's thinking was we were too damned big," Pearce said. "Roger's thinking was that we had to be everywhere. And we were too big. It's just not manageable. She understood the challenges of managing such a large organization."

The first target was Southeast Asia, the same market where managers wanted $1 billion for new models. In February, GM said it would close a plant in Indonesia, where the company had less than 1 percent market share and where Japanese automakers are dominant. The company's push with the Chevy Spin small van lost $200 million in a year and prospects for profits weren't very good.[2]

That started the downsizing. The first big move came in March when Barra brought down the curtain on GM's presence in Russia. The US and European Union had put heavy sanctions on the Russian federation after its president, Vladimir Putin, annexed the Crimea from Ukraine in 2014. The sanctions led to a collapse of the ruble's value. Since GM imported half of its cars in the market, most of its offerings would either be overpriced or unprofitable. Ammann said GM didn't see the political climate getting better, and it was a challenging market to begin with. So Barra announced the closing of the same plant in St. Petersburg that she had a hand in opening less than a decade earlier. That would end sales of all Opel models and most Chevy models. The company would still sell high-end vehicles like large SUVs, Corvettes, Camaros, and Cadillacs, but all that would remain would be a retail operation selling luxury models and sports cars to oligarchs. GM was out of Russia as a mass-market car company.

"We've been reviewing our global operations over the past couple of years," Ammann told reporters at the time. "We're perfectly willing, if we don't see a really good business case to invest somewhere, to make the tough decision and move on."

Russia was just the beginning. In the summer of 2016, Barra flew to GM's headquarters in India. She told Stefan Jacoby, a former Volkswagen executive GM had recruited for its international operations, that a planned $1 billion investment in the market might be a bad bet. Even if the business made money, the profits on the small, inexpensive models that sold to most Indian consumers would be meager and water down GM's earnings for years to come. Plus, the company had just

1 percent market share. There was room for upside, but building the brand and taking on market leader Maruti Suzuki would require a lot of capital. GM's cars, which were jointly engineered with its Chinese partner SAIC, weren't exactly right for the market and would need to be retooled for regional tastes. Barra didn't shut it down immediately, but it wasn't looking good.

While GM was scrutinizing the India operations over the next six months, Ammann had a meeting during the Paris Auto Show in September 2016 with Peugeot SA CEO Carlos Tavares. GM had owned a stake in Peugeot and had a couple of joint ventures together. Ammann and Tavares were talking about them. When the meeting concluded, Tavares asked Ammann if he had any other ideas.

"As a matter of fact I do," recalls Ammann, with a laugh.

He asked Tavares if he wanted to buy GM's European business. For GM, getting rid of Opel and Vauxhall would be surrendering global prestige, but escaping its mountain of losses would be a blessing. Tavares might be able to make use of it. He took over as CEO of the French carmaker after leaving Renault-Nissan and the shadow of its leader, Carlos Ghosn. Tavares had grown restless under Ghosn. He wanted to run his own company and he even had designs on being the CEO of GM before Barra was hired, or maybe Ford before Mark Fields grabbed a promotion to run the company.

PSA was largely a regional carmaker, doing most of its business in Europe. It lacked the global reach and scale to compete with giants like GM, Ford, Toyota, and Volkswagen. With increasing regulations on vehicle emissions and the looming change to electric drive, Tavares knew that a small automaker would never be able to compete. He was keen to expand into new markets and find merger partners. Buying

GM's European business would be a good start. Tied to Peugeot, there could be engineering and costs savings for Opel.

For GM, everything about owning the business was wrong. In Germany, the Opel brand was dowdy and proletarian. A German journalist once described it to me as the car the local butcher drives. Opels fetched lower prices than Volkswagen, but GM had to pay similar union wages. GM didn't have a lucrative commercial truck business as Ford did in Europe, and Cadillac sold few vehicles in the market, so Barra couldn't rely on luxury-vehicle profits to carry the business. That's why Fritz Henderson tried to sell it in 2009. In a market where every carmaker—American, French, German, Italian, Japanese, and Korean—was competing for the same customers, GM really had half a business.

It had shown signs of improvement. Akerson had pulled Chevy out of the market to focus on the Opel brand on the mainland and Vauxhall in the UK. Cost cuts had helped get to about breakeven. The new Astra compact was selling well, but a couple of key happenings made the business almost untenable. First, European emissions standards were getting much tougher, which meant GM had to spend a fortune to make Opel compliant with regulations on the mainland, Ammann said. And when the Brits decided on Brexit, Barra and Ammann had had enough. GM made cars in the UK and on the continent and shipped them both ways. The vote to leave the EU hit the pound hard, making the flow of cars and parts into the UK costly. GM would have made a small profit in Europe that year, but Brexit's currency whipsaw cost GM $300 million, pushing the region back in the red.

Still, even after years of rework, all GM had done was shave down losses. The business still wasn't fetching the kind of returns Barra wanted. And it would require billions for new vehicles to keep consumers interested and a lot of investment to meet ever-tougher clean air rules. Ammann also made the case to Barra that it just took too much of their time when there were more pressing needs.

"It wasn't just financial, like how much we spend in Europe," Ammann told me. "Think about how much time and leadership we spend on Opel, just a tremendous amount of energy on the hope that one day we'll stop losing money. If you believe that there will be some gut-wrenching amount of transformation of technology-driven, consumer-driven things, we have to focus our financial resources and bandwidth that will put us in a position to be ahead of the future, not behind it. That was the general mindset."

After Ammann found an interested buyer in Tavares, GM had an escape hatch. Barra and Tavares bargained for a couple of months to hash out a deal. Ammann and GM CFO Chuck Stevens were holed up with their staff in the windowless basement office of a Paris law firm working for Peugeot. The two GM executives put tremendous pressure on their staff to get the deal done quickly. No one wanted it to leak out early. A deal like this was politically perilous. Merging French and German carmakers would send their unions into a panic, and both would immediately pressure politicians to make sure the deal preserved jobs in their countries. No one wanted the press to get the story before they could manage the politics.

On a Monday evening, February 14, my European colleagues and I heard rumblings that something was in the works. We made a few calls and by 9:00 p.m. I got a tip that Peugeot was negotiating to buy Opel and Vauxhall from GM. Early the next morning French officials confirmed talks were taking place. GM was cutting a deal to get out of Europe. Negotiations went on for more than two more weeks, with a key issue being who would handle the pensions of retired

Opel and Vauxhall workers. Tavares was looking to leave as much of that baggage with GM as possible. If Peugeot could get Opel's plants, dealerships, and sales, but leave retiree obligations with "Generous Motors," he could make the business work. It could be a huge win.

While the two sides haggled over the numbers, Barra and Ammann met with German chancellor Angela Merkel's staff to assure them that finding a new home for Opel was in the best long-term interests of the brand, the plants, and the engineers who worked at the company's complex in Russelsheim, Germany, south of Frankfurt. Tavares did his part, saying that he was open to keeping a separate Opel management team. In the end, Merkel was willing to gamble on Peugeot. And why not? GM was such a poor steward of Opel for so many years that she was bound to find a better home with someone else, almost anyone else. Even a French rival.

In early March, the two sides announced a deal. It was a costly one for GM, but the long slog in Europe was finally over. Tavares got Barra to take a heavy pension load in the deal. GM basically paid Peugeot to take its European business. It was announced as a purchase with the French carmaker sending $2.3 billion to GM. But that just offset the big pension load GM was keeping. GM would give the French carmaker $2.9 billion to cover future Europe pension obligations and keep $6.8 billion worth of plans for existing retirees. GM would be paying $400 million annually for fifteen years to fund the German and UK retiree plans, but that was better than losing more than $1 billion a year on the business and having to spend money on super-efficient vehicles to meet tougher regulations.

For GM's old guard, it was a staggering admission that the company would never be the GM of the 1960s that was a major force everywhere in the world. It was over. For Henderson, it was consolation that the move he tried to make in 2009 was the right one and that members of his board that opposed the Opel sale—led by Girsky—were wrong. For others, Barra made the wrong move. Tim Lee, one of her early mentors, sent her an email saying the exit from Europe was a mistake. Barra's reply: "Decision made. We're moving on," Lee told me.

It was a very bold stroke. GM had been there since the Great Depression. At certain points, like the 1990s, Opel and Vauxhall were very profitable; the money made there offset losses in the US. But it had long gone sour. Opel's German engineers didn't like being told how to make cars by Detroit, a fact that was not helped by Opel's parade of American finance guys running the European business from an office in Zurich, Switzerland, instead of the Russelsheim engineering center. The Swiss office closed in 2009. Opel made progress before bankruptcy with Henderson and later with Girsky running it, but it was still a drag on profits and would need more investment for years. Barra had seen enough.

When looking at the globe, they didn't stop with Opel. If GM was getting out of Europe because the losses were big and she didn't see a quick route to recovery, why should India get a pass? They began wondering whether India was truly so different from other emerging markets, which require billions of dollars in investment just to sell small cars that generate slim profits. As she was selling Opel, she also decided to scrap the $1 billion investment in India and to halt sales of Chevrolet in the market altogether just two months after the European deal was announced. Using the same logic, the sharp-penciled engineer-turned-manager decided to pull out of South Africa as well.

Then she started taking down her operations Down Under. In October, GM closed its Holden plant in South Australia and stopped manufacturing vehicles in the market. That was a painful move for many. Holden was a storied brand. Aussie buyers liked fast, brawny rear-drive cars just as Americans did. Lutz had grabbed the Holden Monaro coupe and turned it into a reborn Pontiac GTO in 2003. The car's jelly bean styling was very 1990s, but it could lay down rubber and it gave Pontiac a much-needed jolt. Reuss made a similar play a decade later. In 2013, GM took the Holden Commodore, a fun-driving and roomy four-door, turned it into a real wolf-in-sheep's-clothing beast of a sedan, and sold it as the Chevy SS. Gearheads loved it. Reuss had run the Holden operations in 2008 and 2009. Barra's design chief, Mike Simcoe, was an Aussie who had led Holden's studio before coming to Detroit. Simcoe and Reuss had an emotional attachment to it. But GM couldn't make money there. By 2020, Holden would be shuttered for good.

Barra's overseas downsizing was just about complete. She had exited Europe plus two of the former BRIC emerging markets that multinational companies all tried to exploit for profit. Remember BRIC? Brazil, Russia, India, and China. In the '90s, anyone who was anyone had to be there to show a growth story. But for carmakers, only China was a moneymaker. In the three years she had run GM at that point, Barra had sold or closed thirteen overseas plants and walked away from five markets that sold 2.6 million vehicles annually.

"We're here to win," Barra said at the time. "We aren't going to win by being all things to all people everywhere. It's not the right strategy."

Jack Smith, the retired GM chairman who led the company in the '90s and was the last CEO of GM Europe to make real money, said in retrospect that Barra's moves were the right call. The company spent a lot of time and money trying to be the largest in the world and make all of those outposts bear fruit. It was just too big to manage.

"She's very capable and she has done some things that I would never have done," Smith said. "As I look at it in hindsight, they were good moves. We were in a lot of places with small market share and not doing well and she got rid of them. I wouldn't have done that. She did."

Smith said that old GM wanted to be everywhere, but often didn't have the cash or the commitment from top management to invest in those markets. He said India was a prime example. GM stuck its toe in the water, but Smith's good friend Osamu Suzuki went in big, forged a partnership with India's Maruti, and became the country's top player. The same thing happened in other small markets, Smith said.

"We weren't doing any business in some of those places," he said. "I give her a lot of credit. I root for her all the time."

CHAPTER 7

⚡

AN ALL-ELECTRIC FUTURE

As GM hacked away the dead wood and cut costs, profits began rolling in. In 2015, the company reported record net income of $9.7 billion. The next year profits were nearly as good, and revenue hit a record $166 billion. The cost cutting was working, and a strong economy and Reuss's fresh models were helping sales. That's when GM started looking to invest more aggressively in electric vehicles.

The first seeds of truly converting the company from a producer of gas burners to an EV maker were being planted. During 2016, when Ammann was president, he wanted to get a view of GM's entire product portfolio for every market, every brand, and every engine. That way, GM could further prioritize its spending on new technology. He wanted a dedicated room where the entire product plan was laid out on the walls, year by year. They found a room in an unused building at the Tech Center in Warren, Michigan, and called it the bat cave because the walls were painted black.

Ammann wanted a visual view of the entire product portfolio. The idea was that he and Reuss, who was running product development, could look at the entire global family of engines and transmissions to see if GM truly needed them all. Despite years of winnowing down the sets of hardware GM used to make its vehicles, there still was some redundancy. Plus, the world was changing; older, less efficient engines had to be scrapped or improved to meet tougher emissions rules.

"We set up this thing we called, unimaginatively, the portfolio zone in this building in Warren no one was using," Ammann said. "We had how many vehicle programs we were doing and how many different powertrain configurations and how much money are we spending doing the next generation of powertrains and compliance. It led to a portfolio that Mark and I ran."

Ammann said that led to another round of rationalization and cuts. Powertrains are big-ticket items for carmakers. They require a lot of up-front investment for the hardware, and emissions testing and certification costs can be massive. By leaning up its portfolio of internal combustion engines and transmissions, GM could save billions on future product programs.

"That was another way to enable resources for investing in electrification and so forth," Ammann said. "It wasn't just, let's get out of Europe, it was, let's streamline the whole thing so that we can then be in a position to do X electric vehicles by Y year."

That gave GM more financial freedom to plow money into electrification. One result was what GM called BEV3 at the time. It was GM's third-generation electric-vehicle battery and would eventually be called Ultium. The second-generation battery powered the Bolt.

"We wouldn't have the firepower to push ahead on BEV3 if we were doing all these other things," Ammann said. "There was a lot of pressure on what's the most amount of money we can afford to spend on everything. Once we figured out how to afford it all, that's when it started."

The next question was how many vehicles and how fast? Barra and Reuss sat down in the summer of 2017 and took a hard look at the company's future vehicle plans, especially plans for electrification. Regulations for carbon emissions got tougher every year. The costs to keep them in compliance just kept rising, Reuss told me in April 2019.[1] To give consumers the big, powerful SUVs they wanted and meet tougher regulations, carmakers were using hybrid systems that paired small electric motors and gasoline engines. They were adding turbo chargers to smaller engines to generate the power of a big engine but with better fuel economy and lower carbon emissions. Carmakers were also paying up for lightweight metals to lean up their vehicles. By 2025, the average vehicle in the US will need to get about forty-six miles per gallon and will cost a lot more to build than it did in 2017.

Even if Donald Trump watered those rules down, which he pledged to do, GM wasn't convinced that he would win reelection. A Democrat would simply reinstate them. Plus, California had an exemption from federal rules. New York, Oregon, and most New England states followed its lead. Trump was trying to eliminate California's exemption to set its own emissions rules, a move that Barra supported. But he could fail with his lawsuit against California or lose in 2020, so it might not matter if Trump decided to throw Detroit a bone. A big chunk of the most populous states would rule differently, and it never made sense to make clean cars for coastal states and guzzlers for the rest. California's rules really drove the market when it came to fuel economy and clean air.

Regardless of what Trump wanted to do in the US, the world had decided to start moving on from fossil fuels. China was mandating electric cars in big cities like Shanghai and

Beijing, where GM had a big customer base. The company pulled in $2 billion a year in profits from China. There was simply no way GM could hang on to its top position in the market without an electric vehicle strategy. And given the cost of batteries, you needed global scale to make it all work. In other words, GM had to make a big commitment to electrification.

Said Ammann of Trump: "It was evident the direction he was pointed was the opposite of where the rest of the world was headed."

The only question was how big of a bet to place as the company got started. Timing will be everything with electric vehicles because the economics are so difficult. If a company tools up factories to make too many batteries and EVs and the buyers aren't there, it's a recipe for losses. Move too slowly as buyers run to plug-ins, and it's a recipe for lost customers as Tesla and other rivals move more swiftly lure them in.

At that point in 2017, the cost to build an electric vehicle was prohibitive. To get a passenger car to be able to run more than 300 miles on a single charge, which is still less than the 450 that most internal combustion vehicles can go, meant that the vehicle needed a seventy-kilowatt-hour battery. That's what Tesla's pricey Model 3 has in its long-range version. At the time, an EV battery pack cost about $270 per kilowatt-hour, according to Alix Partners. That means the battery alone was almost $19,000. That doesn't even count the electric motor, power electronics, and inverter cost. An internal combustion engine, transmission, and fuel system was less than $7,000 a vehicle.

However, making that same gasoline vehicle so it would comply with future rules was rising all the time. A hybrid system could add easily $1,000 to the cost of a vehicle. That alone wouldn't get larger vehicles to 46 mpg, so carmakers were adding more technology and lighter materials. A Chevy Volt, which had more electric power on board, was far more expensive than that. As battery costs fall below $100 per kilowatt hour and gasoline compliance costs rose, their cost curves were headed toward a collision. The intersection of those two cost curves was an inflection point when gasoline no longer had a cost or profit advantage, Barra told me. They weren't there in 2017, but that's the way things were headed.

EVs also have the advantage of removing a lot of other parts, like transmissions, fuel tanks, filtration systems, exhaust tubes, and catalytic converters that used pricey precious metals like platinum, palladium, and rhodium to strip out smog-causing oxides of nitrogen. That would reduce some costs to help even up the economics with conventional cars.

Throughout 2017, Barra was getting more comfortable with placing a big bet. She and Reuss discussed how GM could start developing a larger lineup of electric vehicles, how much it would cost, and how to make it more profitable. The strategy would be built around Bev3, which would be branded as Ultium.

That September, the design team put its panoply of show cars out for Barra and her team to inspect under the company's brightly lit metallic design dome at the engineering center. They had sedans, SUVs, sports cars, a pickup truck, and autonomous shuttles for ridesharing, all built using the BEV3 battery pack. When fitted up with an electric motor, an inverter, and four wheels, the battery pack made up the platform of a vehicle that resembles a skateboard.

"The purpose," chief designer Mike Simcoe told me later, "was to show that we could reuse the electric vehicle architecture and make vehicles that run the gamut."

Building a variety of model types on the same platform would greatly lower the costs of producing a full line of EVs and give GM a crack at what eluded Tesla at that point: a profitable business in electric cars. It would also give GM a variety of vehicles to build and cater to tastes in the US and China so the company could collectively get more sales volume and drive costs down. Ultium's battery technology may be no better than most others. Its benefit is industrial. It's a Lego set that can electrify the entire GM global lineup.

Battery-powered cars had captured the imagination of wealthy, tech-minded drivers. Tesla was the first to tap into that, becoming a hot brand in the process. Its cars began stealing customers away from the likes of Mercedes-Benz and BMW. But in 2017, when Barra was weighing up her own plug-in play, EVs were still only about 1 percent of car sales. They were still too expensive for most consumers and even at fat prices, they lost money. EVs sold by Tesla, GM, and Nissan could take hours to charge and only Tesla models could go more than 300 miles on a charge.

GM had been working on electric batteries and developing vehicles that would run on them. In no way was Barra flat-footed. But spending billions on cars with an uncertain group of buyers was seen as speculative and risky. Internally at major car companies, there were still voices saying that EVs were a costly science project. They assumed Tesla would run out of cash one day and carmakers could carry on as they always had.

Internally, GM was weighing uncertain demand for EV sales against the risk that Tesla and Germany's Volkswagen group and even Ford would capture the buyers who made the switch. That threatened to completely reset customer loyalties and shake up the industry. Tesla already sold most of the electric vehicles on the market. Elon Musk threatened to upend the auto industry the way Apple's iPhone did to '90s mobile phone kingpins Nokia, Motorola, Ericsson, and Siemens. GM's future hinged not only on Barra's courage to make a move, but also on her being wise enough to get the timing right.

Caution was understandable. At the time, Tesla was by far the top seller of electric vehicles with 100,000 sold globally and losses of about $2 billion on sales of its Model S sedans and Model X SUVs. Those Teslas typically sold for more than $100,000 apiece, which is triple the price of the average gas-burning family SUV. With Tesla's $100,000 cars losing money, the challenge for companies to make a buck selling EVs was daunting.

GM knew it all too well. In the 1990s, the company had sold the famous EV1, an aerodynamic two-seater priced at $34,000 that was leased to EV enthusiasts from 1996 to 1999. That was an expensive car back then. GM spent $1 billion developing it and would lose more money selling the vehicles, said Wagoner in an interview. I remember seeing a presentation for the car at the Detroit Auto Show in 1997. GM's then-vice chairman, Harry Pearce, talked about electric cars like the EV1 and also about hybrids that ran on gasoline engines and electric motors. For GM, it was a display of what the company's engineers could do and a glimpse of the future, he told me. But it would be decades before it would be a real business.

The EV1 would bring GM serious credibility with environmentalists, but after leasing 1,100 of them, the company lost a lot of money. A few Hollywood actors like Ed Begley Jr. leased one and promoted it as often as he could. Francis Ford Coppola had one, and when GM ended the program and demanded that lessees return the cars, he refused to give it up and kept it. The company crushed all the cars that it had leased after retrieving them, which then made GM a pariah with the same environmentalists who loved the car.

The economics of electric cars weren't very good twenty years later. Chevrolet started selling the Bolt in 2016 and lost a whopping $9,000 on every one of the $38,000 plug-in cars it sold. Before that, GM sold the Volt plug-in hybrid, which uses a gasoline engine and an electric motor in tandem to get forty-two miles per gallon. The Volt lost even more. Those nasty numbers would drive serious resistance to electric cars inside GM and at other major carmakers, too.

One big reason GM sold the Bolt was to meet government regulations. In California and a dozen coastal states that followed its lead, automakers had to sell electric vehicles or other super-efficient cars like hybrids to be able to sell their profitable gas guzzlers. Selling green vehicles earned ZEV credits. GM could also buy ZEV credits from Tesla, which many automakers did. But that just meant that they were helping fund Musk's effort to eat their lunch.

In the EV race, Tesla already had the advantage of a tremendous amount of investor patience for Musk's losses. Even though Tesla lost $2 billion that year, his company's market capitalization ended 2017 with a total value of $52 billion. That was just $4 billion less than GM's even though Barra brought in near record profits that year. In other words, the market would continue to fund Musk's money-losing operation, but Barra had to fund her own vehicle development with profits from the very gas guzzlers she was seeking to replace.

That put GM and the mainstream car companies under pressure from three sides. Shareholders wanted profits from pickup trucks and sport utility vehicles. But in the car market, Tesla was stealing buyers, gaining a technological advantage in battery development, and building an Apple-like brand for making the cars of tomorrow. Meanwhile, governments were putting the squeeze on with new clean-air rules.

Before Tesla came around, GM also hoped the Bolt, and its predecessor, the Volt, would give the company a greener, high-tech image. In the early 2000s, Toyota branded the Prius hybrid as the cleanest car on the road. It got more than fifty miles per gallon and became the auto industry's standard for new technology. Eventually, Toyota would sell more than 200,000 a year. Honda had also sold hybrid versions of its cars.

While the Japanese were basking in the green glow of fuel-efficient technology, GM had bought the Hummer brand from military contractor AM General and turned its Humvees into a gas-guzzling, commercial phenomenon. That vehicle and its other large SUVs and trucks brought in massive profits but were a target of green lobby groups for being pollutive. Former GM vice chairman Bob Lutz, a darling of the media for his quick wit and endearing braggadocio, had famously called global warming "a crock." GM was viewed by environmentalists and some policymakers as a Luddite among carmakers. In the imagination of educated coastal consumers, GM was the company that killed the EV1 and sold the 9-mpg Hummer, and later needed a government bailout to slip out of bankruptcy. Toyota made the Prius and printed money and now it was Tesla that was making the rest of the industry look bad.

Ironically, Lutz championed the Volt. He was tired of seeing Toyota get all the accolades for its engineering prowess. In terms of technology, it ran like a true electric vehicle until the battery ran down. Then a gasoline engine would kick in and recharge the battery. It leapfrogged the Prius technologically and was a big interim step toward true electric cars. It also helped GM restart the electric-vehicle program and battery lab that had developed the EV1.

GM expanded the battery lab to develop the Volt and had been adding in-house expertise. I toured it for the first time in 2008. There were half a dozen big stainless-steel vaults where GM was testing the Volt's 6-foot-tall, 435-pound T-shaped battery in all kinds of conditions. GM kept the lab and had expertise in-house. They just needed a bigger project and some vision to make use of the resources they had.

At the lab, GM also worked on its own battery chemistry. As the company cut traditional engineers in 2018, Reuss was hiring battery experts and software engineers. That change would prove to be hugely important. Vehicle batteries are packed with lithium, cobalt, nickel, and copper. Those elements are about 60 percent of the cost of a battery, which is why it is so hard for carmakers to make money on EVs. Anyone trying to lower costs has to change the chemistry to reduce the amount of lithium and cobalt. Engineers were already working to reduce cobalt to reduce costs.

All of this meant that GM had some of the tools if the company wanted to sprint to catch up to Tesla. All they needed was the derring-do to make it happen. Doug Parks, who worked for Reuss in product development, was putting together a team to develop some of the vehicles that Simcoe's designer team had dreamed up. Reuss was planning to announce maybe ten of them that would be coming out globally in the next decade.

Reuss wanted to announce a planned commitment to go electric in October. But GM had not yet firmed up a plan for how many electric models the company would develop for the U.S. market, what the list would include, and when they would start selling them. At that point, anything announced would be as much an internal mission statement to rally the company as it would be a public commitment to bring new EVs to market. The battery was in development, but not much work had been done on individual vehicles. Barra met with several people from her communications and marketing staff in the summer of 2017 to discuss the message. The idea was that the auto industry's success in delivering the freedom of personal transportation across the globe had unintended consequences. Smog, carbon emissions, congestion, and accidents all were nasty side effects of this love affair with the automobile. Electric cars would free the world from two of those ills. Self-driving vehicles would reduce accidents and could also alleviate congestion if they were shared vehicles. Ray Wert, a former editor for the irreverent auto website Jalopnik and head of GM's technology communications at the time, was there. So were two Chevy marketers, Joe Jacuzzi and Steve Majoros, Wert said. They pitched the idea of plugging GM's technology push under the banner idea of "a world without crashes, emissions, and congestion." Barra liked the idea and after some discussion simplified it to, "Zero crashes, zero emissions, zero congestion." That would be the external message. Inside GM, they just referred to it as "zero, zero, zero" when talking about the next phase of GM's transformation.

Then the big question was, how many vehicles should GM commit to selling? And how should GM frame its move into electric drive? GM's product plan was in flux, but the company had the potential to announce a pretty big slate of plug-in models that would go into production in the next few years if Barra could get buy-in from everyone involved. Or they could be more conservative and say they were planning just a few, giving the company the future option of backing off if they didn't think consumers were ready. Mike Ableson, who at the time was GM's chief strategy officer, had a meeting with Barra, Ammann, Reuss, sales and marketing vice president Alan Batey, electric vehicle chief Doug Parks, and other company leaders at the end of September. The intent was to discuss the rollout of electric vehicles and how to present it to the world. Should GM expand its plans and go big? And if so, what message should the company send to investors and consumers?

They kicked ideas back and forth about how many they should publicly commit to selling. Some wanted to stretch out the timeline so they could claim more electric models were coming, thereby giving the press bigger numbers for headlines. Batey argued that they should be conservative in their promises because EVs weren't selling in big numbers yet. The main idea was to announce ten EVs and plug-in vehicles globally by 2022. Many of those were for China, where GM was already developing some models to meet regulations. That meant GM would only reveal a handful of real EVs for the US.

"It was the natural tension between the here and now and current earnings versus investing for the future," Ammann said. "It's easy to say we're going to make the quarter and make the year instead of spending money on things that are uncertain and years away."

Some people in the meeting agreed that ten vehicles globally by 2022 was too few. And it would have been at that point. By 2022, Tesla might have more models for sale in the US than GM was announcing. Others weren't sold on the idea that the market was ready for EVs, despite the fact that Tesla's revenue had grown 55 percent that year. Toward the end of the meeting, Wert argued that GM should make a much bigger push, announce more models, and go with the story line that "GM believes in an all-electric future."

It's a great line. It could start to change GM's image by committing to ending carbon emissions. It would show Barra and the company committing to a push for leadership in clean transportation. To do it, the company needed to actually believe in an electric future. There was just one big problem. Almost in concert, Barra said, "I'm not sure we do." And Ammann said, "But we don't," Wert recalls.

The meeting broke up with no conclusion. Tony Cervone, the head of communications, walked up to Wert after the meeting. He told him that if he wanted to get the company to commit to an all-electric public relations campaign, he needed to get to Reuss. It was going to be Reuss's press conference next week and he would develop the product plan with Barra that would prove GM's commitment. Wert walked to Reuss's office on the thirty-ninth floor of the Renaissance Center. Batey was in there chatting with Reuss, and left him waiting for forty minutes.

When Wert finally got in there, he told Reuss that GM should commit to a big plan, and talk about every electric car in the works and said that he thought the time was right to really push the agenda. GM needed to plant a flag and say that it stood for technology and for solving all the problems caused by internal combustion. Reuss was keener on the idea than the others. Here was a GM lifer with a passion for racing who loved Corvettes and Camaros and had gasoline in his veins, and he was open to going electric. He had seen what the design staff could do and knew that the world was changing. Reuss also loves cool cars, and EVs are faster than anything powered by gasoline.

While they were talking, Barra walked into Reuss's office and saw him chatting with Wert. She asked the two of them if they had figured out what would be said at the press conference next week. She turned to Reuss and asked him if he believed in an all-electric future.

"Actually, I do," Reuss replied, saying that he thought it would give GM a simple, straightforward mission that the company could focus on. Since the end game is zero emissions, they should do just that. Barra said that she had thought about it since the meeting and liked it.

"If you're in, I'm in," Wert recalls her saying to Reuss.

The two of them agreed and GM started building a specific plan. Later, the product development staff put together the portfolio of twenty models they could build by 2023. With that plan, GM made its first big commitment and laid the groundwork to eventually go all electric. Granted, some of the twenty models would be rebranded versions for different global markets, but it was still an extensive lineup that would be a broader plan than Tesla's and rivaled only by those of Volkswagen, which is a global powerhouse but one with a minimal presence in the US.

This was a seminal moment for GM's move into the electric age. If the company announced such a commitment publicly, there would be almost no going back. Not only would it be an embarrassment, but the stock price would take a beating. Investors were rewarding Tesla. In the market's view, the jury was in and electric vehicles would be the future and were a growth strategy. Selling internal combustion vehicles was a long, slow road to oblivion. Any company that wasn't making an electric bet was looking less and less relevant to investors.

GM could have gone with a more modest plan rather than take a big gamble on a huge family of electric vehicles. In 2017, there was no consensus on how quickly electric cars would find buyers. Fiat Chrysler CEO Sergio Marchionne was still publicly saying that EVs were money losers. Rival Toyota was also on the fence about battery-electric cars and thought hybrids were the way to go until hydrogen-powered vehicles were ready.

"They made that call," said Josh Tavel, who runs GM's electric truck program. "They looked at hybrids. But those are just 'tweeners. They thought in 2030 it will be all EVs. So let's just get there."

Five days later, on October 3, a rainy Tuesday, Reuss announced the plan at GM's tech center north of Detroit. The press conference was bereft of the usual fanfare, which was unusual given the grave importance and massive strategic move GM was making. Reuss huddled with about twenty journalists at GM's design dome, the same place where

Simcoe had shown eighteen possible electric vehicles to the top brass.

There was one key aspect of GM's strategy that Reuss had unveiled. The company made a calculated decision to build a new platform that would be dedicated to electric vehicles. While they were developing the battery and electric drive system, competitors like Ford, VW, and Korea's Hyundai were putting batteries into vehicle platforms that were originally designed for internal combustion vehicles. They wouldn't carry as much battery power as GM's vehicles would, but they could get to market faster. That meant others could have a new EV for sale first, but GM would have an edge in the long run because they could more easily develop a large portfolio of electric vehicles. GM's plan to commercialize a battery and develop a family of vehicles would start a tortoise-and-hare race with other major carmakers.

"General Motors believes in an all-electric future," Reuss said. "Although that future won't happen overnight, GM is committed to driving increased usage and acceptance of electric vehicles through no-compromise solutions that meet our customers' needs."

He showed three vehicles, crossover SUVs for Buick, Cadillac, and Chevrolet. Under tarps, we could see the silhouettes of the other concept cars. There were sedans, sports cars, a shuttle, and a pickup truck.

Reuss also showed the battery pack, which would be the foundation for the company's entire EV play. It was a large platform about six or eight inches thick that would serve as both the floor and the power storage for GM's future EVs. It would eventually be called the Ultium battery and would be the basis for the entire EV strategy. He explained that they could make many vehicles off that pack, which had the power storage built into the chassis like a skateboard. Different types of cars and trucks could be dropped on top of the skateboard. He had another surprise. GM wouldn't lose money on these vehicles and they would sell 1 million globally by 2023.

"These vehicles will be profitable," Reuss said.

While Reuss was showing the cars and what would be the Ultium battery, Barra put out her own blog post on LinkedIn. She staked out GM's position with her "zero, zero, zero" pledge. GM would target zero accidents and zero congestion with self-driving cars. She laid out a claim to change transportation forever.

"We'll move relentlessly and irreversibly to a zero-emissions future," Barra said. "No more gas. No more diesel. No more carbon emissions."

CHAPTER 8

BLOODY MARY

One of Mary Barra's boldest moves came on Sunday, November 25, 2018, while most Americans were watching football, eating leftover Thanksgiving turkey, or getting over a food coma from the holiday weekend. Five years into her tenure as CEO, she was known as an affable and capable leader of America's largest automaker. She didn't rock the boat with bold statements or proclamations, the way Detroit's legendary car guys once did. But she had steered a once-bankrupt American icon to fat profits and had cut away a lot of bad businesses around the world. Sales were increasing as the economy recovered, and she had navigated GM out of the ignition crisis. Selling Opel was a bold stroke—and it impressed Wall Street—but at that point Barra's big moves had been half a world away. At home, she hadn't yet shown the world that she was the one to break the family china.

She would start grabbing more notoriety that day. Barra called a meeting with UAW leaders and her two top manufacturing executives, Alicia Boler Davis and Gerald Johnson, along with top labor negotiator Scott Sandefur. There were also a handful of attorneys. From the UAW, President

Gary Jones and Vice President Terry Dittes and some of their staff members gathered. The GM team told union leaders that a major restructuring would be announced the next morning, with a threat to close five plants, four of them in the US. Two were small transmission factories in Baltimore and suburban Detroit. The other two were big, historic assembly plants. Lordstown, Ohio, was on the block and the so-called "Poletown" plant that straddled the line between Detroit and the ethnically Polish enclave city of Hamtramck. That was Barra's old plant. A plant in Canada was also threatened with closure. Thousands of jobs would be cut.

The UAW was stunned, Dittes told me. They had no idea there would be closings, not with GM raking in strong profits and auto sales holding near historically high levels. What was worse, Dittes said, is that union members had been making concessions since before the financial crisis and GM bankruptcy. With negotiations set for the next year, workers at GM's plants had told their leadership that they expected raises and better benefits for entry-level factory workers. They wanted to claw back concessions made in years past, not give up more jobs.

"We were beside ourselves," Dittes said. "We had an absolute fit. I won't repeat the things that were said. It probably wasn't very professional. We were blindsided by the whole thing."

Dittes said GM's leaders told him that they had too much production capacity and that they didn't have enough model lines to keep all of its plants profitable. He shot back that GM had plants in Silao and Ramoz Arizpe, Mexico, that could be shut down. The Silao plant makes big pickup trucks and sells most of them in the US. Build them in Ohio or Michigan, they said.

"I told them they have enough product lines, they're just in the wrong country," Dittes said. "We've encouraged them to shut down truck lines in Silao and Ramos and put the work here because this is where the product gets bought."

That evening, the news started leaking out in Canada. The Toronto *Globe and Mail* reported that Barra would be closing GM's oldest assembly plant in North America, the sedan factory in the lakeshore town of Oshawa, near Toronto. The plant had been running since 1953 and 3,300 workers still counted on it for their livelihoods. GM had been building vehicles in Ontario since 1918. As word traveled from the newspaper to the newswires to the Internet, Canadian politicians and Unifor, Canada's union for autoworkers, started frantically calling their contacts at GM.

"I got a call that morning from the news in Toronto saying that GM was going to announce closure of Oshawa," said Jerry Dias, the fiery president of Unifor. "I said it doesn't make a stitch of sense, but I knew I'd be talking to GM in an hour. I said to GM, 'You better not be calling me to close Oshawa.' The frustration was that they were closing five plants and not one was in Mexico."

Unifor put out a foreboding statement: "There is no product allocated to the Oshawa Assembly Plant past December 2019." In the lawyered euphemisms of labor relations, "unallocated" meant no work. No cars to build. Job cuts likely, and maybe a permanent closing of the plant. More ominously, reports said that Oshawa was part of a bigger series of plant closings that would include factories in the US. That stirred the US media.

GM was caught off guard by the leaks in Canada. The company had hoped to alert Canadian and US government officials—in particular the Trump administration—before telling employees and the media. But the fracas in Canada blew the entire plan, which would have political consequences for Barra.

The automaker's government affairs people had informed the
Trump administration but didn't really have a story that would
soften the blow of job cuts.

The next morning, Dias put out a note publicly saying
that he refused to accept the Oshawa plant's closure and
would work to find a way to convince GM to keep it open.
Dias had been active in Canada's labor movement for four
decades. He had a thick shock of dark hair puffed up a bit
like Elvis Presley's coif. He was forthright and sometimes
bombastic, a true believer in the cause of the workingman.
Dias would later resign amid allegations that he breached
his union's constitution. He penned a missive and fired it off
to the media: "We deserve a fair share of the jobs and better
treatment."

Canadian autoworkers voiced their displeasure first, with
Unifor workers walking off the job that morning when the
news was official.[1] That was the first sign that Barra's work to
transform GM would meet serious resistance from labor. Dias
told his members that he intended to make GM deliver on its
contractual obligation to keep the plant open until the fall of
2020 and press the company to use it well beyond that.

Unifor would later run ads at the Golden Globe Awards
and in Detroit's newspapers, challenging the company for cutting American and Canadian workers while adding employees
in Mexico. In ads wrapping the print editions of that Thurs-
day's *Detroit Free Press* and the *Detroit News*, Unifor was blunt:
"US and Canadian workers made GM. Why should our jobs
go to Mexico? Keep our plants open." Inside the paper, there
were more ads: "GM has made excuses for closing five plants
in Canada and the US. But really it's about moving our jobs
and our products to Mexico." And "GM, if you sell here, you
have to build here."[2]

"We got very aggressive," Dias said. "We had wildcat strikes at suppliers and shut down GM headquarters. We ran ads at Golden Globes and Academy Awards. We spent millions. They were making record profits. That was the insulting piece of it. GM says they build where they sell. That's not true. They sell more in Canada than Mexico."

In the US, Congresswoman Debbie Dingell, spouse of the late congressman John Dingell and a former GM executive, got a phone call from a local radio station asking about the closure of the Poletown factory. Dingell didn't know what to say. She had not been notified of the plan. "I didn't believe it," she told me later. "I didn't even think GM could legally close plants in the middle of a labor contract."

They technically couldn't close any US plants. The labor agreement all but prohibited plant closures during the life of the deal, which didn't expire until September of 2019. But GM could stop the assembly lines, lay off the workers, and—in a bit of legal legerdemain—label the plants as "unallocated." For a car plant, "unallocated" is like a cancer diagnosis. The patient isn't necessarily terminal, but the odds of survival aren't good.

At the time, layoffs were unheard of. The economy was roaring, with unemployment a paltry 3.8 percent. Economists call that full employment, which means that everyone who wants to work has a job or may just be waiting out a seasonal layoff. The US auto market had slipped from its all-time high in 2016, but just by a little. Americans were still buying near-record numbers of cars and trucks. Most of them were expensive and highly profitable SUVs and pickup trucks.

Later that Monday morning, as the Detroit press corps filed into a conference room at GM headquarters, we were told that Barra would cut 8,000 white-collar workers, too. This was a new look for Barra. Her public persona hadn't been remotely like that of "Neutron" Jack Welch, the famed General Electric CEO who cut 112,000 workers in his first four years. For the college-educated staffers at GM's headquarters and engineering centers, it was shell shock. Barra wouldn't address the staff in person about the restructuring for three more months. They would be sweating it out into 2019.

The press release was perfunctory, and clearly aimed at Wall Street analysts and investors. The changes, it noted, would preserve $6 billion in cash by reducing costs by $4.5 billion and cutting capital expenditure by $1.5 billion a year. "The actions we are taking today continue our transformation to be highly agile, resilient and profitable, while giving us the flexibility to invest in the future," Barra said in the statement. "We recognize the need to stay in front of changing market conditions and customer preferences to position our company for long-term success."

Not that anyone looks to press releases for comfort, nothing says empathy like a cash flow discussion. The release just said 15 percent of salaried staff, including contractors and workers at several plants. That tallied up to 14,000 job cuts and rippled through headlines on TV and across the web with superlatives like "biggest restructuring since GM's bankruptcy."

Barra then came down to talk to the press. Her explanation made business sense. "We are taking these actions now while the economy and company are strong," she said, adding that GM was facing a "fast-changing industry with fast-changing market conditions. We hope you see that the management team is committed to acting with a sense of urgency."

The optics were terrible. Here was another CEO cutting thousands of jobs right before the holidays and talking about how great cash flow would be once those people were off the payroll. This was coming from a company that had only survived thanks to US taxpayers, who had staked GM $51 billion in 2009 and lost $11.2 billion on the deal. From 2016 to 2019, Barra had made $66 million as CEO. GM had also bought back $14 billion in stock and paid its shareholders $2 billion a year in dividends. Wall Street loved the restructuring and GM stock rose almost 5 percent that day, but no one in Washington would defend it. On the right, President Trump was instituting protectionist trade measures in hopes of creating blue-collar jobs. On the left, presidential hopefuls Elizabeth Warren and Bernie Sanders were decrying CEOs and billionaires for getting rich at the expense of working families.

Barra simply didn't seem like the kind of CEO who would pull the trigger on mass layoffs in rosy times. In person, she is unfailingly upbeat and always optimistic. She usually wears a welcoming smile and has well-rehearsed lines about creating the best products for her customers and value for shareholders. A typical Barra line is one she gave to *Stanford Magazine*, the publication of her alma mater. "We're going to have beautiful, innovative designs. We're going to put the right technology on the vehicle by [consumer] segment, the way the customer wants it," she said in a 2011 interview.

She spoke often about her "zero, zero, zero" vision of GM leading the auto industry into a future. She also spoke of wanting to make those technologies available to everyone, not just wealthy consumers.

Barra did plenty of media interviews, but reporters in Detroit's experienced press corps grumbled that she rarely opened up. I found her to be thoughtful and expansive in a one-on-one setting, but at the podium or in a media roundtable, at this point in her tenure the default was to stick to talking points. That didn't go over well with reporters who were used to the blunt, often controversial pronouncements of retired GM vice chairman Lutz. Former CEO Fritz Henderson had also been an open book when he explained step-by-step to the media how GM would get through its 2009 bankruptcy. Ford Motor Company scion Bill Ford kept up a congenial persona of company patriarch and could be quite engaging with a round table of reporters. Chrysler in the 1980s had a smooth-talking salesman of a CEO in Lee Iacocca, who famously crowed after Chrysler repaid a federal bailout: "We at Chrysler borrow money the old-fashioned way. We pay it back."

Barra's actions said much more than snappy one-liners. The Lordstown and D-Ham plants were especially galling for the union leaders and local politicians. Michigan and Ohio are swing states and carried political implications for both parties. They both also had historic significance. Closing the Hamtramck plant after less than forty years would be a huge slap in the face to 1,400 families who were forced to move to make way for GM.

"There's a sense of betrayal," Hamtramck's Democratic mayor Karen Majewski said. She tried to reach Barra, but her call went unreturned.[3]

If closing Hamtramck sparked bitterness, closing Lordstown would provoke all-out war. That part of eastern Ohio had already seen decades of tough times with steel mill closings. Its people had warmly received Donald Trump in the presidential election two years earlier in part because he pledged to bring manufacturing jobs back. After Big Steel's decline, GM and its suppliers were the only remaining big industrial employers.

The politics got ugly fast. President Trump called Barra the day of the announcement to voice his anger over the closing of Lordstown. He demanded that she find a way to keep it open and then he took to the airwaves. "They damn well better open a new plant there very quickly," he said in an interview with the *Wall Street Journal* the next day.[4] Canadian prime minister Justin Trudeau was more polite. He went on Twitter to say his government would do everything possible to help families affected by the production cuts at GM's factory in Oshawa. He added that he'd called Barra "to express my deep disappointment in the closure."

Democrats leaned on GM, as well. Congressman Tim Ryan, a young Democrat whose district included Lordstown, wrote, "We fought together to keep GM afloat and the American taxpayers bailed them out when they were on the verge of bankruptcy. And in return, GM has turned their back on us when we need them the most. This is a bad combination of greedy corporations and bad policymakers with no understanding of economic development."

Another prominent Democrat, Ohio senator Sherrod Brown, also went after the company. "GM received record tax breaks as a result of the GOP's tax bill last year, and has eliminated jobs instead of using that tax windfall to invest in American workers," he said in a statement.

Part of GM's political problem was inevitable. Politicians always hate layoffs. But part was self-inflicted. GM's Washington office didn't have a story for the Trump administration to be able to explain what was coming. They also didn't alert all the lawmakers in key states where layoffs would happen. Some were caught completely off guard by press reports.

That's not the only way the communication was bungled. The company's planners had a good idea which plants were to close and how many workers would lose their jobs. They even had a plan to offer transfers to all of the 3,000 Lordstown workers whose current jobs would be eliminated. If they were willing to move, they could continue to work for GM by making Corvettes in Bowling Green, Kentucky, or making trucks in Indiana, Missouri, or Flint, Michigan. GM had work for any laborer who would move. There was also a plan to possibly keep the Hamtramck factory open. It was penciled in as a potential site to build future electric pickup trucks and SUVs. At that time, it was impossible to tell how quickly consumers would embrace plug-in vehicles, so it was hard for GM to tell the union how many employees would be needed. But the factory had a chance.

GM had not fully formed its EV plans. If D-Ham was on the block but offered job security during 2019 labor contract negotiations, it would look like GM had come around on job security issues and made a concession. Company negotiators were going hard at it. If they took Hamtramck away and gave it back during talks for a new contract that summer, it made GM's offer look sweeter. That way the UAW wouldn't try to cash in after years of little or no raises. Said one staffer in GM's Washington office: "They were so focused on driving a hard bargain with the unions that they lost track of the politics."

Lordstown was a much different story. Its future was on much more perilous ground. Presidential hopeful Joe Biden tried to firm up his cred with factory workers by assailing GM in a speech to the International Brotherhood of Electrical Workers in Washington. "There used to be a basic bargain in America— you guys know it better than anybody—it said that if you're a part of building the success of an enterprise, you got to share in the benefits," Biden said after the plant idled its assembly line. "Not now. If an enterprise is hit hard, it used to be everybody took a hit: the CEO, the managers, the hourly workers."[5]

Elizabeth Warren called the move corporate greed at its worst, and Bernie Sanders railed against GM for slashing jobs while hauling in record profits. Later, Michigan representative Debbie Dingell said GM had become "the most hated company in Washington."

Internally, Barra's image as a perpetually upbeat leader was changing. She was looking more "hard-core," one long-time GM engineer told me at the time. Over the next couple of months, white-collar workers feared that they could be among the 8,000 people who would be fired. All through December, January, and part of February, employees wondered when they might get a call from human resources and have to clean out their desks. Rumors spread through GM's various engineering and administrative offices that almost any Friday or Monday would be the day security would start walking people out.

Meanwhile, managers were combing through the salaried ranks to see who was expendable. The cuts sometimes had little to do with performance or ability; it was about cash preservation. Bigger salaries sometimes got the axe. In engineering, some of the cuts were made because GM was getting rid of some of those who worked on internal combustion vehicles. As the months passed, the anxiety and gloom among the staff intensified.

"I wish they would just do it and tell us who is going," complained one anonymous employee on the pages of a rogue website, TheLayoff.com.

In early February, the culling began. It started piecemeal at first as GM managers went through different parts of the company. Employees would get an email or Skype message that summoned them to a conference room for the bad news. In some offices they gave the laid-off workers a reusable blue bag to take items to their cars. In some departments, the blue bags became emblems of the firings. Once word got out, people feared seeing them.

When the cuts were finally done, Barra took the stage on March 5 in the cavernous lobby of GM's vehicle engineering center. It was a standing-room-only crowd, with many employees gathered on the ground or on a walkway above her. Thousands more tuned in via an internal webcast, carried around the globe. In a thirty-minute presentation, Barra said that GM faced both near-term problems and existential challenges. She said the company needed to cut back on weak businesses and ditch anything that didn't make solid returns. GM could no longer afford to prop up parts of the business because of old-time inertia or the pride of being the biggest. Their priorities had to be trucks and SUVs that print money today and new technology that would lead GM into tomorrow.

Barra tried to prepare the remaining staff for a dramatic transformation in transportation. Electric cars and self-driving vehicles would bring about a new kind of business, and GM had to move now, she said.

"We need to seize this opportunity," she told the crowd. "Make no mistake, we are not here just to compete in this new world . . . we are here to win."

For Barra, it was about survival. GM would either be disrupted by the likes of Tesla and Google or it could get in the game and even try to retake the lead and do the disrupting.

"Once you start to believe in the science of global warming and look at the regulatory environment around the world, it becomes pretty clear that to win in the future, you've got to win" with electric and driverless vehicles. "This is what we really believe is the future of transportation," she told me in the weeks after the cuts were finished. She added that GM was finally going to start to grow again, reversing decades of decline.

Barra's analysis was right. The world was changing. While GM was finding its feet after bankruptcy and wrangling with a big recall, it had fallen behind. Tesla was the leader in electric-vehicle technology and was building a powerful brand behind the cult-like admiration for Musk. Germany's Volkswagen AG was beginning to emerge as a fast follower with battery-powered cars. Google was years ahead in self-driving car software. Apple had a mysterious skunkworks team called Project Titan that was rumored to be a foray into the car business. The last thing Barra needed was to blow money on internal combustion vehicles with poor margins and an ancient global empire that lost money. She gave plants and models in the US the same stringent test.

She saw a threat to car ownership as we know it. Uber and Lyft were showing people a different way to get around. If even 10 percent of people gave up on car ownership in favor of on-demand rides from Uber, Lyft, or Google's Waymo, carmakers would face a profit squeeze. At a private presentation to a Wall Street analyst, she was asked how many car companies might exist in twenty years. "Maybe five," she replied. "Maybe zero."

The events of late 2018 showed the world her foresight, toughness, and cold pragmatism. Even when many of her own engineers and managers thought that electric vehicles and self-driving technology were many years away from transforming the industry, she saw that it was time to move. She also learned from the old GM, which had drifted into bankruptcy over several decades by waiting until a crisis arrived to make big moves. Old GM never managed to get out ahead of its problems.

GM is far smaller now, but its more focused lineup of models and leaner workforce make it a profit machine. Before Barra's cuts, the company was using a little more than 80 percent of its production capacity. That had always been a magic number with car companies. Make your plants run at more than 80 percent and you make money. More than 90 percent and these companies generate a princely cash flow. But below

that 80 percent line, a car company can bleed red ink. Profits were rolling in by 2018 because GM was selling so many
expensive pickup trucks and hugely profitable large SUVs like
the Chevy Tahoe and Cadillac Escalade. Loaded up, some of
those can generate tens of thousands of dollars in profit per
unit. GM was also pulling in about $2 billion a year from its
Chinese operations. Net income of $8.1 billion was the com-
pany's second best at the time.

Behind the great numbers, Barra saw trouble. By September 2018, US sales were off more than 5 percent, despite the
fact that carmakers had amped up rebates and low-interest
loans to move the metal. China had also seen its first decline
in auto sales in two decades. Since those two markets were
GM's top sources of income, Barra had reason to worry. Times
were still good, but there was no growth to be seen.

With electric cars and self-driving vehicles, she also saw
a path to growing GM after decades of downsizing. Most city
dwellers in places like New York and San Francisco relied
on public transit, cabs, or rideshare. They didn't buy many
cars, and when they did, they were partial to Japanese and
German brands: Toyota, Honda, BMW, Mercedes. But if GM
could beat Silicon Valley to developing self-driving cars, or
at least get in the game before other established automakers, Barra envisioned a new business that served those coastal
commuters who rarely bought cars. With self-driving taxis,
GM could make regular consumers out of all of them. Barra
and Ammann dreamed of reaping profits that were fatter than
what the company made building cars.

Barra explained to me that she was aiming for nothing
short of a real transformation for GM, potentially its final
transformation. That meant no plant, brand, business, or
nameplate was safe. Lordstown was one such place. The
plant had been building the Chevy Cruze compact. Small

cars were in favor when gasoline was $3.50 a gallon in 2013. But by 2018, gasoline was about $2, and Americans once again embraced SUVs and pickups. They didn't just prefer them; they abandoned small cars and sedans altogether. Lordstown had gone from running on three shifts to one shift, which is a recipe for bleeding cash. The same logic applied to the old plant in Hamtramck, which built the Chevrolet Impala and Cadillac CT6 sedans. Both were also out of favor, despite the CT6 being one of the best luxury cars GM had ever built. Both models would be killed off as part of the restructuring.

Killing the Impala was a big move. The car has been a slice of classic Americana since the 1950s. It was America's family car for decades. I learned to drive in my dad's '85 Impala wagon. It was rear-wheel drive and I had to navigate the heavy snows of upstate New York. With snow tires, it managed all right in some deep drifts that we'd get from December to March. It was our family car until the minivan was born..

As late as 2007, consumers bought more than 300,000 Impalas in a single year. Gwen Stefani had a classic yellow 1961 Impala in her "Hollaback Girl" video. Ice Cube has a '63 Impala and likes to pose with his gold-painted classic. But in 2018, sales of the Impala had sunk to just 56,000. GM couldn't afford nostalgia.

"If we don't take the steps to keep the company healthy for not just the next few years but the next few decades, then shame on me," said Barra.

Leaders who move as fast as she did, especially women in a notoriously macho industry, meet tremendous resistance. Union workers were irate, with talk of a potential strike getting louder and louder in the spring of 2019. GM paid its union workers well but had also put more production in Mexico than any competitor. UAW's Dittes said that union workers were already fed up with making concessions almost nonstop for more than a decade while the company hired more Mexican workers. With GM's profits growing, there would be no way to get a contract ratified if GM didn't give something back.

Throughout that summer, the fate of the four US plants that Barra planned to close became a top story in Motown, even at Detroit Tigers games. The company was preparing to start selling its all-new Chevy Blazer, which revived a storied name that had been killed off in 1994. The small but athletically styled Blazer SUV carried the same rugged image as Ford's rival Bronco. Starting at just $31,000, it should have been a hit with working-class buyers in the Midwest. But the Blazer would be assembled in Ramos Arizpe, Mexico, the same plant where GM had made the Pontiac Aztek almost twenty years earlier. The fact that the original Blazer was previously assembled in the now-shuttered union plant in Janesville, Wisconsin, already roiled the union.

"The new Chevy Blazer is hitting showrooms, which is exclusively built in Mexico. It is my hope that every single UAW member or family member not purchase this vehicle unless it is made in the USA by the members of the UAW," Dittes tweeted in January 2019.

Chevy's marketing team decided to put the Blazer atop the General Motors Fountain, which stands above the centerfield wall at Comerica Park. GM has had Corvettes, pickup trucks, and SUVs above that waterfall, reminding the Tigers' faithful that GM is the big carmaker in town. If someone belts a home run to dead center, there is the Chevrolet Fountain on ESPN and other major networks, with gushing water below the vehicle of choice for national audiences to see. But now it was apple pie, baseball, and a Mexican-made Blazer.

Detroit's ABC News affiliate published a poll asking if GM should put a Mexican-made SUV atop the fountain. Union workers lit up a local radio call-in show raging about it, call-ing it an insult. It was especially thorny in Lordstown. Dan Morgan, then chairman of the closed plant's UAW Local 1112, tweeted a picture of the vehicle—which he had hoped would be made in his plant—and wrote simply, "It's bullshit!" GM took the Blazer down before a single pitch was thrown in 2019, replacing it with a Silverado pickup, which is built in plants in Mexico, Flint, and Fort Wayne, Indiana.

Political pressure was escalating. Union workers were angry and had political cover from Trump and from Demo-crats. Lordstown was "one more symbol of the broken prom-ises that this president has made to workers," according to South Bend mayor Pete Buttigieg at the Democratic debate held in Detroit. Congressman Beto O'Rourke made a stop in Lordstown and posted a video online while meeting with the UAW local's president, David Green. "I've met with these members of the UAW who are striking outside of facilities in Cincinnati, in Lordstown, Ohio, which has just been devas-tated, decimated by GM and their malfeasance," O'Rourke said at the same debate. "What they want is a shot."

If the UAW's new president, Gary Jones, needed a green light to take the union out on strike, he had it. He also had pressure to do it. Jones and other UAW leaders were under investigation by the Justice Department for stealing funds from the Chrysler Training Center and the union's own cof-fers. GM executives were sure he would strike just to distract his own members from the investigation. Chrysler and UAW labor negotiators were later convicted for giving union leaders gifts and cash perks. GM sued Fiat Chrysler saying they used graft to buy off the union to get an unfair advantage. Jones and his predecessor, Dennis Williams, both were later sent to prison. Dittes told me that he called the strike against GM and that it had nothing to do with Jones's investigation.

Even if Dittes called the strike, union members were still wary of leadership. With the UAW's reputation looking worse with every arrest and indictment, the negotiators facing off with GM, Ford, and Fiat Chrysler would have to get a good contract in 2019 to show members that they were working on their behalf.

Just before the contract deadline, Barra had offered the union $7 billion in investment in eight different plants and 5,400 new jobs. There were also significant pay raises. Hamtramck would be given a new lease on life with the assignment to build electric vehicles once GM started rolling them out. But it wasn't enough. Union workers were on the picket lines Monday morning.

"Going into this bargaining season, our members have been very clear about what they will and will not accept from this contract," Dittes said the day the strike started. "We are standing up for fair wages. We are standing up for affordable, quality healthcare. We are standing up for our share of the profits. We are standing up for job security for our members."

I met up with him that morning on the picket line in front of the Hamtramck plant. The union wanted to keep Poletown, Lordstown, Baltimore, and Warren, Michigan open. GM also had thousands of temporary workers in the plants, and the union wanted them to be given full-time status, benefits, and a path to the top pay scale of more than $30 an hour.

The only thing GM offered Lordstown was a plan to sell the plant to a little known and thinly funded startup that wanted to make electric pickup trucks. If the startup, called Lordstown Motors, even survived it would employ a fraction of the plant's GM workforce. The union would have to organize the workers there all over again. They refused the deal.

Barra's showdown with the union would be ugly and expensive. The strike was costing the company more than $40 million a day. Even worse, GM was in the process of getting its all-new Chevy Silverado and GMC Sierra pickups ready to sell. The strike halted that new-truck launch cold and would delay it for forty days. Meanwhile, Ford's F-150 and Fiat Chrysler's new Ram pickup were stealing customers of GM's most profitable product line.

As the weeks passed, the rhetoric got increasingly nasty. Dittes put out a letter, saying, "GM is purposely stalling the process to starve its workers off the picket lines. These delay tactics have a human cost. Families are suffering." GM's lead negotiator, Scott Sandefur, countered with his own letter, accusing the UAW of stalling.

On October 15, with the two sides finally getting closer, Barra met Dittes and Jones at the bargaining table in a conference room in downtown Detroit. Barra offered to give all temp workers a path to full-time employment within four years. Workers would get raises and $11,000 signing bonuses, and Hamtramck would be dedicated to making electric vehicles. The deal was close enough to what Jones needed and was something he could get his members to ratify to end the strike. The 3,000 or so in Lordstown would oppose this deal, but the others would like the short runway for temps to grow into full-time worker status, plus the significant bonus and raise package. Union leaders agreed.

Barra got to close three US plants, but it was expensive. Once the union ratified the deal, GM was racing to boost production and get trucks to its dealers. No one knew it at the time, but just as production was catching up from the strike, the Covid-19 pandemic would shut plants down again. Thanks to the strike, GM went into the pandemic with the thinnest inventory of any player in the hotly contested truck market. All told, the strike cost GM a whopping $3 billion and left behind a lot of anger among employees.

Barra kept Hamtramck open as an electric truck plant, giving it a new lease on life. Oshawa also got work, first making aftermarket parts and later assembling pickup trucks. Dias said he believes the social pressure the union put on GM made a difference.

"We went from the outhouse to the penthouse," he said.

It was tough for Barra personally. As a plant manager, she tried to build strong relationships with union workers. Her father was a UAW member and the pay and benefits he earned provided her family with a solid, secure lifestyle.

"My teeth are straight because of the UAW," she said.

Politically, Barra would also pay a hefty price as Donald Trump would make her a frequent target of Twitter tirades and political rants when he was on the stump. She stuck to her plan.

"It's hard when you're the focus of all the criticism. You have to stay steadfast," Barra said in an interview a few months later, when I asked about the blowback from her transformation plan. "One of the things I learned in the bankruptcy is, if you have a problem or a challenge, it never gets better over time. You have to address it. Once you know what you need to do, you need to do it."

CHAPTER 9

⚡

WRATH OF DONALD TRUMP

Barra's trouble with Donald Trump started before he was even inaugurated. Shortly after he won the election in November, GM had canceled a shift in Lordstown and cut 1,200 jobs because Cruze sales had slowed. The company was also making a hatchback version of the car in Mexico. Trump didn't respond at the time, but on January 3, with his oath of office in less than three weeks, he tweeted out a warning shot to GM.

"General Motors is sending Mexican made model of Chevy Cruze to US car dealers tax free across border," he tweeted. "Make in USA or pay big border tax!"

In truth, GM was sending very few of the Mexican-made Cruze to the US. The company's plant in Ramos Arizpe shipped about 5,000 a year north of the border, a tiny portion of sales. Americans hate hatchbacks. Trump didn't care about those details. He wanted GM to make that version of the Cruze in Lordstown, Ohio, to give that factory better job security. For a plant whose demand dropped from 300,000 cars a year to less than half that, the hatch wouldn't save anyone's job. But imports were one of Trump's big issues and he would put tremendous pressure on carmakers to bring production to the US.

During the 2016 campaign, Trump successfully courted union voters by telling them that he would bring back the American spirit of manufacturing things. He would be on their side, not that of Wall Street big shots. He promised to slap tariffs on foreign-made products and tear NAFTA up by the roots. He also said he would end US involvement in the Trans-Pacific Partnership, which was a proposed trade deal with Australia, Brunei, Canada, Chile, Japan, Malaysia, Mexico, New Zealand, Peru, Singapore, and Vietnam that was meant to give members leverage against China. Unions and American workers saw it as a NAFTA for Asia and another way to export jobs. Trump had also promised to get rid of the lopsided trade deal with China, which had been crafted to give Chinese imports a cheap and open path to American consumers.

Workers in places like Michigan, Ohio, and Pennsylvania loved it. Before Trump, it had been decades since either major political party had really connected with downtrodden factory workers. Hillary Clinton talked about green jobs, which meant nothing to coal miners, warehousemen, and autoworkers who drive pickups to their jobs and hunting blinds. Mainstream GOP candidates mostly embraced Reagan-era free trade, which created wealth but also resulted in offshoring high-wage blue-collar jobs. Even if Trump was insincere or unsuccessful in bringing those jobs back—even if he was lying and had no intention of helping them—at least he bothered to talk to blue-collar workers. The upper Midwest bought what he was selling: a pledge to restore the hard-hat prosperity of the '70s. For industrial America, that was the very heart of "Make America Great Again."

Three days after inauguration, Trump invited Barra, Ford CEO Mark Fields, and Fiat Chrysler CEO Sergio Marchionne to Washington. His message was clear: he would cut corporate taxes and eviscerate Barack Obama's tough emissions rules on automobiles if Detroit's Big Three would hire more workers in the US. A simple quid pro quo. Trump calls himself the ultimate dealmaker, and that was his offer Detroit couldn't refuse.

To Barra this offer was simplistic and too out of step with her plan. Trump assumed that the Big Three wanted to gut environmental regulations so they could go back to earning 1990s-era truck profits, without worrying about climate change. He called Obama's environmental regulations "out of control." He promised to get the government out of the way and roll back the previous administration's planned hikes in fuel economy rules. Trump didn't care if the average vehicle on the road got more than fifty miles per gallon in 2025; he thought government rules and regulations were simply an outrageous overreach by government and a killer of jobs.

After that White House meeting, the three CEOs held a quick press briefing. Fields and Marchionne hailed the president for working with the industry. Barra struck a slightly different tone. "There is a huge opportunity working together as an industry with government that we can improve the environment, improve safety, and improve jobs creation and the competitiveness of manufacturing," she told reporters.

Improve safety and the environment? Trump didn't believe in global warming and hated clean-air rules. He wanted jobs, jobs, and more jobs. Even more than most politicians, Trump cared deeply about the twenty-four-hour news cycle and what it meant for his popularity. He promised America a roaring economy and a revival in auto, steel, and coal in the Upper Midwest and Appalachia. And he intended to deliver it. No one, and certainly not *this woman*, would stand in his way. Trump administration officials who were in that meeting said that Barra talked about pushing electrification and new technology that would lead to her vision of a future with zero emissions. They said she didn't read the room and looked naïve, provoking Trump instead of taking a more deferential tone.

In contrast, Fields was happy to play along with the president, saying publicly after the meeting that working with Trump would bring a "renaissance in American manufacturing." Fields had already scaled back a plan to make the Ford Focus compact in Mexico. It was done for business reasons because, like GM's Cruze, the Focus wasn't selling. Trump took credit anyway, tweeting a thank-you note to Fields for canceling Ford's expansion in Mexico: "This is just the beginning—much more to follow." Soon after, when Ford announced a $1.2 billion investment in three US plants—actions that had been in the works for several years—Trump again took credit. "Big announcement by Ford today. Major investment to be made in three Michigan plants. Car companies coming back to US. JOBS! JOBS! JOBS!" he tweeted.

Marchionne also loved Trump's vision. He had no interest in spending billions to develop electric vehicles that he thought would lose money for years to come. His company, even more than GM and Ford, relied almost exclusively on trucks and SUVs to drive earnings. His profits came from Ram pickups and the Jeep line of SUVs. Within a year, Marchionne tooled up a plant in Michigan to make the same Ram pickup trucks that he was building in Mexico and built a new Jeep facility in Detroit. Trump was overjoyed, and Marchionne was happy to let him do a victory trot.

And there was Barra, cutting jobs. When she announced the restructuring in November 2018, Trump called her to complain. Larry Kudlow, the president's chief economic advisor, was also unhappy with GM. He tried to explain in more polite terms that they were offering her a deal and a chance to grow within the US. He told reporters how disappointed the administration was with GM.

"Look, we made this deal, we've worked with you along the way, we've done other things with mileage standards, for example, and other related regulations," Kudlow said. "We've done this to help you and I think his disappointment is, it seems like they kind of turned their back on him."[1]

GM released a statement trying to put out the fire. "We appreciate the actions this administration has taken on behalf of industry to improve the overall competitiveness of US manufacturing," it said.

This wasn't the kind of anger that GM would settle with a press release. Trump was on the warpath and Barra was his target. He was about to thrust her into the kind of spotlight that she disliked, making her a public lightning rod for the anger of his MAGA base.

Ohio was a particular hot spot for Trump. During a July 2017 rally in Youngstown, near Lordstown, he had promised voters that the steel and auto jobs that were lost in recent decades would come back under his reign.

"I rode through your beautiful roads coming up from the airport," Trump told his supporters. "I was looking at those big, incredible once job-producing factories. Melania asked me 'what happened?' I said those jobs are all coming back." The crowd roared with applause as Trump continued. "Don't move. Don't go. Don't sell your house. We're going to fill those factories up or rip them out and build brand new ones. It's going to happen."[2]

Trump said he called Barra about the job cuts, claimed that he gave her a real bollocking. He pressed her to keep the plants in Ohio, Maryland, and Michigan open, especially Lordstown. Barra explained that the market had changed.

The Chevy Cruze no longer sold very well, and they didn't have anything to build there that would keep its workforce busy. She tried to appeal to his business sense, but Trump wasn't having it. He told her that she could move a vehicle from Mexico.

"We don't like it. I believe they'll be opening up something else," Trump told reporters later. "And I was very tough. I spoke with her when I heard they were closing and I said, you know, this country has done a lot for General Motors. You better get back in there soon. That's Ohio."

The next day he kept at it via Twitter, his bully pulpit. He chastised GM for not closing plants in Mexico and China. US and Canadian workers making more than $20 an hour were getting cut, but the Mexican plants that paid $4 an hour were untouched, he ranted. "Very disappointed with General Motors and their CEO, Mary Barra, for closing plants in Michigan, Ohio and Maryland. Nothing being closed in Mexico and China. The US saved General Motors and this is the THANKS we get. We are now looking at cutting all GM subsidies."

Inside GM, her public relations team was hoping to get past the twenty-four-hour news cycle and wait for Trump to find his next target for a Twitter tirade. Barra's top advisors in government affairs and public relations—some of them lifelong Republicans—told her to play nice and let it blow over. But Trump was unrelenting.

In another tweet, he roared, "General Motors made a big China bet years ago when they built plants there (and in Mexico)—don't think that bet is going to pay off. I am here to protect America's Workers!"

At the time, one of GM's spokesmen told me that, aside from badmouthing them on Twitter, there was little Trump could do to hurt the company. The president simply didn't have the authority to target one company with any kind of punitive actions for cutting workers and managing its business. That may be true for most presidents, but not for Trump. He knew exactly how to hit GM. First, he threatened to put heavy tariffs on cars from Mexico, which would hurt GM more than others because the company imported more Mexican-made vehicles than any other company. He also made veiled threats to end the $7,500 per car electric-vehicle tax credits that helped GM sell its Chevy Bolt at an affordable price.

That, too, would hurt GM more than anyone except Tesla. The Trump administration went right after Barra's plan to sell electric vehicles. GM was still benefiting from a $7,500 tax credit given to consumers who bought the Chevy Bolt. Every carmaker could sell 200,000 vehicles and the consumers got a rebate for $7,500 in their tax return. It was a strong incentive for people to buy EVs. Since Tesla and GM had sold more plug-in models than anyone, they would soon run out of credits unless Congress and Trump renewed the program and lifted the cap.

Meanwhile, GM was planning to build EVs in China for the Chinese market. The government in Beijing mandated it. The Trump administration seized on that.

"There's disappointment that it seems like GM would rather build its electric cars in China rather than in the United States," Kudlow told reporters. "We are going to be looking at certain subsidies regarding electric cars and others, whether they should apply or not. I can't say anything final about that but we're looking into it."[3]

During his time in office, Trump would never do anything to raise the cap on plug-in car incentives and renew the tax credit. GM had used most of its credits in past years to sell the Volt. Though the Volt was a plug-in hybrid and did use gasoline, its buyers got credits that counted as one of GM's 200,000 sales using the credit system. That meant that the

Bolt would be on the market without the benefit of tax credits, while models from competitors that went green after GM did would have an advantage.

Early in Trump's presidency, Barra did try to play nice with the petulant commander in chief. Soon after he was elected, Trump's administration had formed a "Business Strategy and Policy" group packed with big-name CEOs, and Barra accepted the White House's invitation to join. Other big names included Jamie Dimon of JPMorgan Chase, BlackRock CEO Larry Fink, Walmart CEO Doug McMillon, Ginny Rometty of IBM, Indra Nooyi of PepsiCo, and retired GE CEO Jack Welch. Another big name: Tesla's Elon Musk. The White House also started an "American Manufacturing Council," which included Musk and Fields from Ford.

At first, many business leaders welcomed these new groups as a chance for corporate America to be "the adults in the room with Trump," as one participating CEO told me. Trump's saber-rattling threats to raise tariffs on Chinese and Mexican goods played well with working-class voters but made traditionally Republican corporate leaders nervous. Free trade and globalization gave them access to cheap labor in the developing world, a global network of tech talent, and markets aplenty for their own goods and services. None of those CEOs wanted to support protectionism, but they had to be careful to stay close to Trump and avoid his wrath.

Trade is one issue where Trump had a real point. Tariffs with China were heavily skewed toward Chinese interests, especially when it came to cars and parts. American vehicles paid a 25 percent tariff going into China, but it was only 2.5 percent coming the other way. Free trade can be a good thing, but it also has to be fair.

Mexico was another issue. Tariffs through NAFTA, which George H.W. Bush negotiated and Bill Clinton signed, were more fair. But despite creating lots of industrial jobs in Mexico, wages in factories stagnated. That was, in part, due to the fact that the Mexican government under the Institutional Revolution Party, or PRI, controlled its largest union, the Confederación de Trabajadores de México, or CTM. The CTM had been signing contracts at new auto plants for BMW and other new entrants to the country that paid a starting wage of about $1 an hour, which was far less than the starting wage in existing plants. The PRI-controlled union was writing new labor contracts for Mexican auto plants before workers were hired and had a chance to vote on them. Those contracts suppressed wages to draw in foreign investment. Free trade is supposed to create more wealth for all, so Mexican workers can afford American goods and our companies get a new market. But it doesn't work so well if the Mexican government's union syndicate keeps pay rates down. American workers suffered for years under this scheme and Trump's US Trade Representative Robert Lighthizer knew it. That's one reason his team pushed for a new deal that required more than 40 percent parts content made by employees at $14 an hour to get the low tariffs on Mexican-made goods. That would result in more US and Canadian parts going into Mexican-made products that are destined for the US.

Corporate leaders wanted to stay close to the president to make sure populist actions didn't upend their businesses. A series of brazen moves tested their resolve to be both good corporate citizens and friendly with the president. The first came on January 27, 2017, when Trump made good on his campaign promise to crack down on Muslim immigration by banning refugees from seven majority-Muslim nations. The move set off a firestorm. There were protests at Uber, Google, Facebook, and other tech companies. Uber was hit hard because some of its technology developers and many of its drivers are immigrants. Employees took to Twitter to complain and sent a hail of emails pressuring CEO Travis Kalanick,[4] who sat with Barra on Trump's Economic Advisory Board. He resigned under duress.

Barra stayed on the board. So did Elon Musk, but he tweeted to his adoring followers: "The Muslim ban is not right." He quickly deleted that tweet and others,[5] but he explained in a statement that he preferred to stay on Trump's committees to try to engage the president and change his policies.

"I believe at this time that engaging on critical issues will on balance serve the greater good," Musk wrote.

Ford chairman Bill Ford Jr., the great-grandson of company founder Henry Ford, openly disagreed with Trump. He spent a weekend chatting with CEO Mark Fields about Trump's Muslim ban. The company's hometown of Dearborn, Michigan, was home to the largest Muslim population in the US. In the shadows of Ford's headquarters are three mosques, including the massive Islamic Center of America. Many of Dearborn's Muslim residents work at Ford. On February 3, Bill Ford and Fields issued a statement saying, "Respect for all people is a core value of Ford Motor Co., and we are proud of the rich diversity of our company here at home and around the world. That is why we do not support this policy or any other that goes against our values as a company."[6]

Sticking by Trump would only get tougher for American business leaders. In June, he pulled out of the Paris Climate Agreement, which was to pave the way for nations to reduce carbon emissions and fight climate change. Obama had promised America would sign on, along with 187 other nations. Trump's exit from the deal put the US on a short, inglorious list that included Iran, Turkey, Iraq, Angola, Libya, South Sudan, and Yemen.

That was more than Elon Musk could take. He was making the world's best-selling electric cars and selling solar panels for residential housing. His entire business model was built around freeing the world of carbon emissions and the bonds of Big Oil. "Am departing presidential councils. Climate change is real. Leaving Paris is not good for America or the world," Musk tweeted. Three hours later, Disney's Bob Iger did the same, tweeting, "As a matter of principle, I've resigned from the President's Council over the #ParisAgreement withdrawal."

This was a chance for Barra to make a stand, to give herself and GM's brand a halo that showed that the company stood for being a part of the solution to climate change and the electric future she wanted to lead. Musk built a cult-like brand doing just that. She had just started selling GM's first electric car in seventeen years, the Chevy Bolt, and had pledged an "all-electric future." At this point in 2017, many people who bought electric cars did so out of principle. They loved technology, but many also believed that global warming was the most serious issue facing the planet, and that the gasoline burning in our cars is a key culprit. They loved Musk's determination to tackle the problem.

Rather than join Musk by walking away from Trump and standing up for her vision, Barra hung in there and passed on the opportunity. On June 2, the *New York Times* ran an editorial that took the CEOs to task for staying on Trump's committees even as he parted ways with the Paris Accord. Barra was one of three executives (along with IBM's Ginni Rometty and Intel's Brian Krzanich) whose photos were above the headline.

"Many prominent business executives have advocated for policies to address climate change. They've made the case not just on environmental grounds but on commercial ones, saying that American competitiveness would suffer if the United

States abdicated leadership on climate," the *Times* wrote. "Now that President Trump has ignored that advice and decided to withdraw the United States from the Paris climate agreement, executives who disagree with him ought to stand up for what they believe. Otherwise, they are lending their own credibility and implicit support, and that of their companies, to his environmentally, diplomatically, and economically self-defeating position."

When asked why Barra wouldn't bow out and take a stand for clean air—even as she was planning to push GM as a tech-savvy, green carmaker with electric vehicles—GM handed out a standard press statement. It said that it was better to engage the president and preserve a dialogue. A few days later, when I asked a GM executive why Barra was still present on Trump's increasingly forlorn committees, the executive lamented that it looked like GM didn't stand for anything.

It only got more tense after that. When white supremacists rallied violently in Charlottesville, Virginia, with one of them driving into a crowd of protestors and killing a woman, Trump initially blamed everyone involved while saying that there were "fine people" on both sides. He did condemn the white supremacist groups that were part of the violence, but for the remaining business leaders he had not done enough. His reaction was too tepid at a time when the nation's darkest hatreds were stepping into the light. Walmart's Doug MacMillon wrote in a letter to employees that Trump "missed a critical opportunity to help bring our country together by unequivocally rejecting the appalling actions of white supremacists."[7] Intel's Krzanich, Merck's Kenneth Frazier, and Under Armour's Kevin Plank quit the committees. AFL-CIO president Richard Trumka did as well. Frazier said in a statement: "America's leaders must honor our fundamental views by clearly rejecting expressions of hatred, bigotry and group supremacy, which run counter to the American ideal that all people are created equal."

With American business leaders fleeing the president, Blackstone's Stephen Schwarzman set up a conference call for the remaining CEOs, including Barra, Pepsi's Indra Nooyi, Jamie Dimon, and a few others. All had been outraged by Trump's handling of the Charlottesville mess.[8] Barra expressed her own dismay at the president's comments. McMillon of Walmart and Laurence Fink, the CEO of private equity firm BlackRock, both told the group they were leaving and suggested others do the same. Nooyi also pushed to disband the committee. After that call, Schwarzman told the president that the committee was done. But before they could announce it, Trump used Twitter to claim that ending it was his own decision.

Barra had stayed until the bitter end, even though she certainly didn't agree with Trump. Privately, she has told people at GM headquarters that she was disturbed by his comments and actions. But she was in a tough spot. Her vision didn't match his plan. If she tried to mollify him, nothing she did would ever be good enough. But if she took Trump on, his actions and rhetoric might hurt the company.

Some of her reaction is pure pragmatism. She doesn't get drawn in by discord and she won't risk getting into a public flap that could hurt GM. At the same time, hanging in with Trump didn't really get her anything. Trump had no interest in expanding the $7,500 tax credit given to consumers who buy an electric vehicle, which would undermine the Bolt. He technically couldn't end the credit system just for GM because it was an industry-wide program that helped any automaker that sold EVs or plug-in hybrid vehicles. But he could just let it fizzle, which he did.

By the fourth quarter of 2018, the Bolt had used the remainder and GM was out of credits. Sales of GM's EV fell from a high in 2017 of more than 23,000 to about 16,000 in 2019, the first year without subsidy credits. Barra was planning to sell other electric models; a big push into EVs was a major part of her transformation plan. GM would need those credits and other government support to grow the market.

Trump also redoubled his war on imported cars and parts. He threatened a 25 percent tariff on Mexican-made cars in February 2019, directing the Commerce Department to investigate whether imported vehicles constituted a national security threat. As silly as that seemed (it's not like we need American-made compact cars to fight a war) Trump could use Section 203 of the Trade Expansion Act to try to do it. It's the same mechanism he used to slap a 25 percent tariff on imported steel. At a minimum, he could drag out the investigation long enough to make automakers rethink any expansion in Mexico. Inside GM, most execs thought that there was no way Trump would go through with it. But they also fretted that, as angry and mercurial as he is, he might just do it. Even a 10 percent tariff would cause GM huge headaches. It made $40,000 pickup trucks in Mexico. A 10 percent tariff would chop $4,000 from the bottom line of one of its biggest moneymakers.

And then there were all those auto parts—30,000 for every car with many of them made by Mexican labor. A 25 percent tariff on parts alone would add $1,800 in costs for a US-made sedan and $2,800 for a pickup truck, according to Toyota North America CEO Jim Lentz.

In the end, Trump backed down and preserved a modified version of NAFTA under a new name, the US-Mexico-Canada Agreement, or USMCA. There were some changes that required more US and Canadian parts content for cars built in Mexico and then shipped north. They were sensible changes but probably not enough to bring back thousands of parts jobs to the US. The threats did temporarily keep GM and others from expanding production in Mexico, until they knew what the Trump administration would do with tariffs.

Trump's changes did make one important change that would later affect GM. USMCA stipulated that the Mexican government had to let workers elect their own unions and oversee fair elections. If workers wanted to remove the CTM, the new government under Andres Manuel Lopez Obrador had to make sure they could do it. The first major election, which would happen starting in 2021, was at GM's pickup truck plant in Silao. Workers there organized their own independent labor group called SINNTIA, which translated stands for National Independent Union for Workers in the Automotive Industry. SINTTIA unseated the CTM in Silao. The new local bargained with GM and got a better compensation package.

That happened after Trump left office. Even though he kept Mexican trade in place, Trump was far from finished with Barra. Doing what he does best, he created a wedge issue, stoking the union's frustration over Mexican-made cars just as labor talks began in the summer of 2019. When the last Cruze rolled off the assembly line in Lordstown, Trump went into attack mode on Twitter.

"Because the economy is so good, General Motors must get their Lordstown, Ohio, plant open, maybe in a different form or with a new owner, FAST! Toyota is investing 13.5 $Billion in US, others likewise. G.M. MUST ACT QUICKLY. Time is of the essence!" Then he directly antagonized Barra in a way that would make union negotiations even tougher for her: "I asked her to sell it or do something quickly. She blamed the UAW Union—I don't care, I just want it open!"

That month, the two talked by phone. Trump told Barra he wanted GM to do something with the plant. The best she could tell him was that GM would try to find a buyer. Trump immediately returned to Twitter to rile up the union and blame Barra: "Just spoke to Mary Barra, CEO of General Motors about the Lordstown Ohio plant. I am not happy that it is closed when everything else in our Country is BOOMING." The tirade continued: "G.M. let our Country down, but other much better car companies are coming into the US in droves. I want action on Lordstown fast. Stop complaining and get the job done! 3.8% Unemployment!"

Then he went straight after the upcoming negotiations and made Lordstown the centerpiece. It didn't matter that it made little industrial sense for GM to save that plant. It was massive and would require several successful models to keep its large workforce busy. Its body shop and assembly lines were set up for a compact that GM would no longer make. It would cost billions to retool that factory for a larger model.

Trump roared: "General Motors and the UAW are going to start 'talks' in September/October. Why wait, start them now! I want jobs to stay in the USA and want Lordstown [Ohio], in one of the best economies in our history, opened or sold to a company who will open it up fast!"

Barra told me later that GM couldn't easily retool Lordstown for larger models. "Think about your house," she told me. "You have a 1,500 square foot house. You want to expand it to 2,000 feet, but you want every room to be a little bigger. You couldn't fit a bigger vehicle through the paint shop and the paint shop was in the middle. You can't have a house and make every room a little bit bigger. It just doesn't work that way. That was the challenge that we faced."

Trump was already pressing the union's buttons, but he took it further by using Barra as his foil when bragging about his economic achievements. Though Hillary Clinton had won union households by 51 percent to Trump's 43 percent, he did far better than Mitt Romney had done against Barack Obama, according to an AFL-CIO exit poll published by the

Washington Post. In fact, he did as well as Ronald Reagan did with union voters during his landslide reelection in 1984. Trump's angry tweets carried weight with union members.

He also railed against GM on the stump. At a rally in Grand Rapids right after GM put the four US plants on Barra's unallocated list, he went after the company. "I'm also fighting with General Motors and the UAW to take swift action on the GM plants at Hamtramck and Warren, Michigan, and Lordstown, Ohio. Get the damn plants open," he said to the crowd.

He kept it up on Twitter for days. "Car companies are all coming back to the US. So is everyone else. We now have the best Economy in the World, the envy of all. Get that big, beautiful plant in Ohio open now. Close a plant in China or Mexico, where you invested so heavily pre-Trump, but not in the USA. Bring jobs home!"

In truth, no one was coming back to the US. Every time car companies invest in an existing factory that will make a new version of the vehicles that plant is already building, they put out a press release that says they are investing in the region. Those announcements just mean they are preparing the plant for a new version of some existing car. It's usually not a new economic development. These news announcements are tantamount to a spouse telling their better half, "Hey, we aren't getting divorced this year." But Trump seized on them to pressure GM to hire in the US.

When the UAW strike began that September, Trump put out a tweet taking both sides to task but focusing on GM as the bad guys. "Here we go again with General Motors and the United Auto Workers. Get together and make a deal!" In a short meeting with reporters the day the strike started, he offered federal mediation if needed, but also took the opportunity to take another swipe at Barra and GM for building more vehicles in Mexico. "We don't want General Motors building plants outside of this country, and we're very strong on that. The UAW has been very good to me. The members have been very good, from the standpoint of voting. The relationship is good."[9]

Even after the two sides reached a deal and the forty-day strike ended, Trump still wasn't happy. At a rally in Battle Creek the next month, he took yet another shot at GM: "General Motors gave us a little hard time with one building, wasn't happy about that. It was the only building I had a problem with in the whole car industry. Right? All right, you know the one I'm talking about. I didn't like that."

It's a grudge that he never let go. Not even when Barra stepped up to help produce ventilators to help the Trump administration manage the Covid pandemic. On March 17, Barra called Ken Chenault, the retired American Express chairman who was heading up an ad hoc group of companies, called Stop the Spread, that were trying to marshal resources to battle Covid. Chenault connected Barra with a small Seattle company that was making a new ventilator, one that could handle multiple respiratory needs in one unit. The product worked, it was smaller than older ventilator designs, and wasn't expensive. Its producer, Ventec, just had too little production. Barra pulled together engineers from GM and Ventec that evening to start talking manufacturing.

When it looked like GM would be able to lend its manufacturing know-how and huge supply chain connections to get Ventec moving, she called Kudlow and gave him the good news. On March 21, GM and Ventec made the announcement that they would start engineering assembly capability to mass-produce ventilators. The move hearkened back to Detroit's role as the arsenal of democracy during the Second World War, when the carmakers converted auto plants to make tanks, trucks, guns, and bomber planes.

"By tapping their expertise, GM is enabling us to get more ventilators to more hospitals much faster. This partnership will help save lives," Ventec said in a statement at the time.

The two companies were working on converting an idle parts plant in Indiana to making ventilators. Barra sent a team of her engineers to Seattle to look at Ventec's components and drawings. GM started contracting suppliers who make small motors for car windows and windshield wipers to see if they could quickly turn out the moving parts for ventilators. Suppliers who made hoses that went in engine bays had to make smaller ones for the 10-by-11-inch VOCSN ventilator. The VOCSN is used for critical-care ventilation. It also delivers concentrated oxygen to the patient and has a nebulizer that sends medication to the lungs, secretion management that creates an artificial cough, and a suction device to keep the patient's chest clear. The eighteen-pound unit replaces fifty-five pounds of equipment.

GM reckoned that its engineers could quickly convert the Indiana facility, which used to make small electrical components, because it had lots of space to set up tables where workers would sit and assemble these devices. Making a ventilator is more like building a watch than assembling a car.[10] Barra set a goal of getting production started in thirty days.

For her, this was a way for GM to give back, to step up in a time of historic crisis and help the nation. It was also a project that would galvanize some of GM's engineers. If they could deliver quickly and be part of a national effort to save people from Covid-19, it could be a galvanizing force in changing GM's culture, she figured.

"Doing the ventilator project was a game changer from a culture perspective," Barra told the Automotive Press Association in Detroit. Before that, "If I told the team, we're going to work with some small company and within 180 days we're going to be making 30,000 ventilators, they would have looked at me like I was crazy. Everyone pitched in and helped. 'Ventilator speed' is something that gave our team confidence."

While GM's engineers were cramming with Ventec's team, Trump broadsided the company with a Twitter attack. On March 27, GM and Ventec had what they needed in place to start getting equipment, plants, and suppliers ready for production. They were just waiting on the Trump administration for an order to go. Then Trump let Barra have it.[11]

"As usual with 'this' General Motors, things just never seem to work out. They said they were going to give us 40,000 much needed Ventilators, 'very quickly.' Now they are saying it will only be 6000, in late April, and they want top dollar. Always a mess with Mary B," Trump wrote on Twitter. He even ordered Barra to make ventilators in the Lordstown plant, which GM had already sold at Trump's behest.

"General Motors MUST immediately open their stupidly abandoned Lordstown plant in Ohio, or some other plant, and START MAKING VENTILATORS, NOW!!!!!! FORD, GET GOING ON VENTILATORS, FAST!!!!!!" he bellowed on Twitter.

Trump invoked the Defense Production Act, which allows the president to compel companies to produce goods needed for national security. He used the act to push GM to do what they were already doing. The company had been working with Ventec before Trump even knew it. GM got production started in thirty days and eventually built 30,000 ventilators for the national stockpile and sold them to the government at cost.

Barra's team got it done. Three days after assailing Barra and the company, the mercurial Trump praised GM. "General Motors is doing a fantastic job. I don't think we need to worry about General Motors," Trump said, speaking highly of the company in two appearances. "They really seem to be

WRATH OF DONALD TRUMP

working very, very hard. I think I'm getting very good reports about General Motors."[12]

Barra reflected on the trouble she had with Trump. She said she had to keep her head down and stay focused, but it was difficult.

"It was hard because a lot of it I took very personally and it hurt. We were working to do the right thing for everyone and that's the responsibility when you're running a large company," she said. "You have to do the right thing. There wasn't a conversation that I had with the former president where I wasn't talking about the importance of the US leading in electrification and the transformation that we needed to do. So I feel I remain true to what the strategy was for General Motors. It was hard to live through."

CHAPTER 10

⚡

LORDSTOWN

Lordstown, Ohio, sits on a twenty-three-square-mile rural patch of land about an hour from Cleveland at the intersection of Interstate 80 and the Ohio Turnpike. Unbeknownst to the workers making Chevy Cruze compacts at the fifty-year-old plant in 2010, they were also toiling away at the crossroads of the auto industry's past and its future. Massive change was barreling down the highway.

When the plant started building the Cruze that year, GM had high hopes for it. Gasoline was expensive and car buyers were snapping up high-mileage compacts. With the Cruze, GM had made an earnest effort to design a car that really could take on Japanese small cars like the Toyota Corolla and Honda Civic. It was roomy and the cabin was nicer than past efforts by GM, which isn't saying much considering the cheap-feeling cloth seats and Hasbro-like plastic the company had used in past iterations like the Cobalt and the woeful Cavalier. The new Cruze felt more expensive than it was. The Eco version of the car got a combined 32 mpg, a shade better than the Honda Civic's 29 mpg.

In 2011, the first year the model car was sold, it beat the best year for the Cobalt, selling 231,000 in the US. It actually beat the Civic in sales that year, though Honda was in the process of redesigning its stalwart compact with a much-freshened version. Still, for a GM that had phoned in its small-car efforts for years, the Cruze was a success. The workers in Lordstown were cranking them out in three shifts and getting overtime. No one in Lordstown sweated job security.

Why would they? That plant had weathered decades of GM downsizing and survived bankruptcy. It didn't employ 10,000 as it did in the 1990s; it was down to one-third that, but it had been a fixture in the community for half a century. When it opened in 1966, the assembly line was cranking out popular cars like the Chevy Impala, Caprice, and Bel Air sedans. Auto industry legend John DeLorean converted the plant to make the Vega compact when he ran Chevrolet in the late 1960s and early '70s. While taking reporters on a tour, he told them that the factory was so big, "you can see the curvature of the earth in here."[1]

When DeLorean retooled the plant, it was the most highly automated in GM's huge archipelago of North American factories, which stretched from Quebec to Southern California. GM wanted to lower costs for its small cars. Workers were pushed to turn out a hundred vehicles an hour instead of fifty-five and complete tasks in thirty-six seconds instead of sixty. They complained bitterly. Cars came off the line incomplete or damaged. Management said workers were intentionally damaging cars. The union blamed the line speed for quality problems.

Upset with how the plant ran, the UAW went on strike in March 1972 for a little more than three weeks, finally getting a deal that slowed the line speed down.[2] The workers got what they wanted, with operations returning to how they ran before. They also came out with a reputation. UAW Local 1112 was hard-core. The plant's young, bearded workers pushed back against management in an activist movement that *Business Week* called "Lordstown Syndrome." That reputation would last decades.

The Mahoning Valley, which was anchored by nearby Youngstown and its steel mills, was prosperous at the time. It didn't last. The region took its first hit five years after the GM strike when Youngstown Sheet and Tube closed a steel mill and laid off 5,000 workers in September on a day called "Black Monday." That was just the beginning.

Foreign producers with newer, high-tech mills and lower wages were pouring steel into the US. When a recession hit in 1982, American steel producers had way too much capacity. US Steel started closing its most inefficient mills, including its Youngstown works, cutting another 5,000 jobs.[3] By 1985, the US saw the number of fully integrated steel mills drop by almost half to twenty-three, and 50,000 jobs were lost.[4] The Mahoning Valley, which includes Mahoning and Trumbull Counties, was decimated. From that point onward, GM's 10,000 employees and all of the parts jobs that fed the plant were all that separated the region from becoming a post-industrial wasteland.

With the Cruze, there was justified optimism. Gasoline prices were over $3 a gallon and got higher every year until 2014. The plant turned out well over 300,000 of the cars that year for the US and Canada. Workers were getting overtime pay and life was good.

But in 2015, things were beginning to change. Gas prices were falling that year and Cruze sales tumbled as well. Consumers started drifting away from small cars and back toward pickup trucks and SUVs. Every month, when monthly sales numbers were reported, the news was about how car sales were falling but SUV and pickup sales were booming.

Behind the scenes at GM, Barra's vision of the company's future was also making the existence of the Northeast Ohio plant rather precarious. The ruthless examination of GM that Barra and Ammann were taking meant that, if Lordstown's small-car business didn't generate big returns, it would be under scrutiny just like the overseas markets that she and Ammann were selling and closing.

It wasn't looking good. Gasoline sank close to $2 a gallon in 2016, the lowest since 2004. Cruze sales dipped below 190,000 in the US that year and GM started cutting shifts at the plant. The third shift got laid off first, sending 1,250 of the plant's 4,500 workers to unemployment.[5]

Dan Morgan, the chairman of Local 1112, started getting nervous. In 2017, he reached out to GM with a plan to make the plant more profitable in hopes that the company would give his union brothers and sisters a new, more popular vehicle to build.

Morgan is a tall, burley, and bearded family man who grew up in northeastern Ohio. He's the kind of dad who posts photos of his son's wrestling match victories or daughter's crowning as homecoming queen on Twitter. The native Ohioan is all in on union ideals and believes in the cause of the working class.

He was calm on the outside but secretly sweating the fact that the Cruze was falling out of favor. He wanted to send a strong signal to GM that his local was open for business and would do what it took to secure another vehicle with a better future. He made a list of changes he would allow in the local contract to make the plant more profitable.

Morgan said he would accept outsourcing of non-assembly jobs like handling of parts and materials to lower-wage workers employed by a subsidiary called GM Subsystems LLC, which paid far less than standard union assembly wages. The union also consolidated two locals in the region to one, which effectively cut in half the number of union officials who drew a paycheck from GM while working at the local hall.

The union also allowed GM to cut the number of skilled tradesmen (including electricians, pipe fitters, mechanics, and die makers) in half to 130, by letting the company contract out for overtime skilled-trade work and by changing job classifications. They also allowed management to send in contractors to repair supplier parts and assembled vehicles at the plant, and to drop the number of extra workers employed to cover absentee workers from 150 to 60.[6]

According to Morgan, GM labor relations managers said that the concessions could help him get the plant a new product, but they made no commitment. Signs weren't good. Cruze sales were down 20 percent and in April of 2018 the company suspended the second shift. That meant another 1,500 workers would be laid off. More ominously, GM offered $60,000 buyouts to older workers, which was a sign that layoffs wouldn't be temporary.

The chairman's fears were realized in November 2018 when the plant went unallocated. No one at Solidarity House in Detroit had any hint of good news for him, either. When I visited the Local 1112 union hall that summer, he was clearly sensing the worst was coming.

"Everything they asked us to do, we did," Morgan said, with deep resignation in his voice. "And we still were unallocated."

Even then, Morgan didn't give up hope. Part of him didn't believe GM would actually close the plant. And even if Barra intended to do it, it was his charge to do everything he could to save it. He also thought the UAW might be able to bargain for a new vehicle to run down the assembly line.

UAW's Terry Dittes said he went into negotiations in the summer of 2019 with an agenda that he telegraphed to GM. He wanted to keep the four unallocated plants open, get pay raises for the existing workers, preserve healthcare benefits, and get temps working in GM plants a path to full-time work.

GM's first offer in September left Lordstown out in the cold, along with the small transmission plants in Baltimore and Warren, Michigan. And it came up short in other areas. The overture also promised a battery plant in Lordstown. The union rejected it and after another day of talks walked out.

Dittes ran up against Barra's tough pragmatic side when he tried to save Lordstown. He tried to appeal to her patriotism and marketing sensibilities. That corner of Ohio, near the Pennsylvania border and not far from Pittsburgh, is where the East ends and the Midwest begins. It's pickup truck country. He tried to get her to move truck production from Mexico back to the US.

"I think you should close a truck plant in Mexico and build products in Lordstown," he told her. "You could be a hero. You could create thousands of American jobs in an area where you want to have product loyalty, in a part of the country where they buy trucks. You would be a superstar."

Barra's mind was made up and she wasn't going to budge.

"We've made those decisions," she told Dittes.

"We're just not done here," he responded. And the strike plodded on.

When the two sides reached a tentative deal in October, Morgan started calling members of the bargaining committee from his hotel room at the Marriott next to GM headquarters. He got the word from Solidarity House that his plant was finished. He sat on the edge of his bed in shock and disbelief. It had been a long shot all along, but he had hoped and prayed to save his hometown's industrial jewel.

"I just felt sick to my stomach," he said. "I really can't believe they're doing this."

With GM would go suppliers like Magna, which made seats for the Cruze. Unemployment went up to between 6 and 7 percent in Trumbull and Mahoning Counties. The US average is around 5 percent. More people in the region were under the poverty line, 17 percent, compared to 10 percent at the national level.

GM's departure alone didn't devastate the region. The collapse of steel did that. And its demise had already sent many people packing, said Arno Hill, Lordstown's Republican mayor. The population of the Mahoning Valley fell from 530,000 in 1970—during the heyday of steel—to about 425,000 in 2021.

Before GM left, Bill Clinton had talked about building a payroll center for the Defense Department in the region. Another developer had discussed an idea for an indoor NASCAR track.

"We're still waiting," Hill said. "We're the land of broken promises. It's just been forty years of going down the tubes."

Closing the Lordstown assembly plant was a knockout blow for his town and the region as anything resembling an industrial center. To Hill, it's not just unemployment that has hit his town and the surrounding areas. The quality of the jobs is nowhere near as good. People had options before the downsizing. They didn't feel like the last remaining employer had them by the throat.

"In the 1970s, if you didn't like working Copperweld Steel, you'd go to Republic Steel or General Motors or Packard Electric," he said. "Or you went to Alcan Aluminum. Now if you want to job-hop you're either a nursing aid jumping from nursing home to nursing home or you work at McDonald's and you're jumping to Wendy's or Burger King."

I grew up in such a place. When I was a kid, Syracuse was an industrial town with a snooty, private college sitting on top of a hill near downtown. General Electric, Budweiser, Miller Brewing, Carrier Corporation, Allied Chemical, New Process Gear, Crucible Steel, and other manufacturers supplied the steel lunch box dads with good union jobs.

When it evaporated starting in the 1980s, poverty swept in. People left. Most of the kids I grew up with went away to college and never returned. They found better jobs in Boston, New York, or hither and yon. Those who stayed were teachers, healthcare workers, or worked low-paying jobs and lived in their childhood home into their thirties.

In Northeast Ohio, people left just to stay employed by GM. The company transferred many workers to plants in Michigan, Indiana, Kentucky, and Missouri. Many just needed to work a few more years to get their pension, then they could move back home.

Some refused to go, like Scott Brubaker. He was a union officer who had worked at GM for twenty years when the plant closed. They offered him a job at the Corvette plant in Kentucky. He worked there for a few weeks, living in an RV. When the strike started, he went back home to picket in front of the Lordstown plant. It hadn't officially closed until after the strike settled.

Brubaker decided the hell with GM. He took a job for around $2 less an hour, clearing trees and land for developers. Eventually, he told me, he and his friend grew the business and were getting work in New York and Pennsylvania. He makes as much or more than he did for GM even in the years when the Cruze plant had a lot of overtime. But he's working for a small business with lousy healthcare coverage. When his daughter got Lyme disease, he had to pay $25,000 out of pocket.

But he isn't going. He's been living on a fifty-acre farm that has been in his family for three generations. These days, he raises cattle and supplies beef to a brew pub that sells grass-fed steaks and burgers. He has landed on his feet, for sure, but he lost his GM pension and gold-plated healthcare.

Many others have scattered all over the Midwest to other GM plants. Dan Morgan, who once was the stalwart leader trying to save his hometown factory, had to pack up and move to Kentucky to build Corvettes. It wasn't easy with two kids in high school, but he didn't see many other options in Lordstown, and with college tuition years approaching, he couldn't risk being out of work or taking a pay cut.

When the factory closed, the town itself took a big hit. Lordstown lost $1 million a year in income tax just from GM, Hill said. That's almost half the 2018 town budget.

"We've cut back on capital improvements," Hill said. "We're doing our best to keep the doors open."

Like a lot of industrial towns that lose huge employers and entire industries, Lordstown is trying to lure in new employers. It's a challenge. They're landing smaller employers who hire fewer people than prior tenants, and at less money. Hill said there are employers coming in, but they aren't employing 5,000 as GM did before it started canceling shifts.

TJX Home Goods is one. The retailer opened a distribution center in the area employing 1,000 people. The initial pay was $14 an hour. The Workers United union came in and organized the plant, pushing starting pay up to $17 an hour. GM pays its veteran workers $32.

Surely someone is thankful to get those jobs, but the damage was complete. The Mahoning Valley lost its grip on the region as a hub for industry. It was now Anytown, USA, trying to lure in distribution centers for retail goods at half the money that auto and steel jobs once paid.

Trump couldn't help them, either. He pressured Barra to find something for the plant to do. The best GM could do at the time was sell the plant for $20 million to an unknown startup called Lordstown Motors. The company's founder, Steve Burns, was a wide-eyed dreamer and entrepreneur who wanted to make the first electric pickup.

At the time of the deal, Burns had one prototype truck and it wasn't anywhere near ready for production. He had spent four years with another Ohio startup called Workhorse Group that had plans to make electric trucks for the US Postal Service. He was trying to push Workhorse into electric pickups and drones. The board preferred to focus on postal vans and the two parted ways.

A former manager who had worked with Burns at Workhorse described him as smart, but also a bit scattered. He was a font of ideas for new businesses and technology but lacked the focus or business acumen to get them to market. In Burns's entire tenure at Workhorse, the company never reported an annual profit.

Dittes said the union didn't give much credence to Lordstown Motors because it had little funding and no buildable vehicles. He thought it was just a way to get Trump off the automaker's case. And largely it was. GM had few options to quickly sell the 6-million-square-foot plant to in quick order to give Trump a press release so he could say he saved the region.

Lordstown Motors looked like it had a chance. In October 2020, the company raised $675 million from an investment fund called Diamond Peak Holdings that was started by real estate investor David Hamamoto, who had no experience in the auto industry. The deal was a reverse merger during a crazed period in 2021 when Wall Street money was pouring into electric-vehicle startups.

Here's how the scheme worked. An investor like Hamamoto would take a small amount of cash and list a public
shell company's stock on the market. Then he would raise
more cash, telling investors that he would go out and scout
an acquisition for a reverse merger. Anyone who put cash into
the shell company, called a Special Purpose Acquisition Company, or SPAC, would be trusting Hamamoto and his team
to do proper due diligence and find a good company. When
he did, they would put in even more money, which would
seed the company with cash, get the SPAC's stock listed, and
instantly have its shares publicly traded.

That means that a startup like Lordstown Motors, which
had no saleable product, zero financial history, and a virtually unknown CEO in Burns would be able to get its shares
listed without going through the grueling road show process
of a traditional public stock offering. On those road shows,
company executives meet with bankers and buy-side investors
and sell them on the company's future. Burns only had to sell
Hamamoto and his team.

While Workhouse had hoped to make electric delivery
vans for the US Postal Service, Oshkosh Defense won the contract. In the four years that Burns ran Workhorse, its revenue
never exceeded $10 million and the company only lost money.

It was SPAC mania at the time. Investors were all looking for the next Tesla, whose shares had soared in value. The
company's market capitalization at the time Diamond Peak
bought Lordstown was $362 billion, which was more than
Toyota and double Volkswagen's value. It was seven times the
value of GM. No one thought Burns was the next Elon Musk,
but there was a craze to invest in electric vehicles. Burns had
a start on developing an electric pickup truck and had bought
the old GM plant, which was enough to get funded during
that period of hysteria.

Trouble started almost immediately. Burns had repeatedly said that the company had orders for 100,000 of its Endurance pickup, which wasn't in production yet. A short seller called Hindenburg Research published a report accusing Burns of exaggerating claims of future sales commitments to customers. The investment firm interviewed former Lordstown Motors employees and business partners and claimed that the orders were "largely fictitious." Burns had even hired a firm to go out and seek preorders, but none of it was binding business.

Burns denied the allegations. In a phone interview, he said that he was clear that none of the orders were binding. He went on CNBC[7] in a television hit from the plant floor, where he was wearing a hard hat. It looked about as convincing as Michael Dukakis's appearance in a tank with an Army helmet on, a move that doomed his presidential campaign.

Longtime CNBC reporter Phil LeBeau pressed Burns on the preorders. He said that they were not binding sales; it was an exercise meant to gauge interest so he would know how many to produce. LeBeau wasn't having it. He reminded Burns that he had called them "serious orders" during a previous appearance on his show and had aggressively characterized the preorders as a strong indicator of interest in the truck.

It was starting to look more like another broken promise. The SEC stepped in and started examining Hindenburg's claims. The company's board also had to have a look. The company had issued a "Going Concern" notice saying that it may not have cash to survive a year. By June, Burns and CFO Julio Rodriguez were out after the board concluded that Burns had overstated interest in the truck.

All is not lost for Lordstown, though. With Lordstown Motors faltering and struggling to get its truck into production, Taiwan-based Foxconn Technology Group signed a deal to buy the plant to make Lordstown's Endurance pickup, another EV for startup Fisker Inc., and to build electric vehicles on contract for any other company that needed production.[8]

And GM? Barra wasn't finished with Lordstown. She may have closed a plant, but she had a plan to bring the town into the electric age. True to her promise from contract talks in 2019, GM announced that it was forming a joint venture with Korea's LG Chem to make battery cells for the Ultium battery packs that would power all of GM's future EVs. The joint venture planned to hire 1,100 workers. It wasn't Lordstown assembly, but it was a lifeline for a region that had lost so much.

Right there on an empty plot next to the Lordstown Motors plant, GM and LG broke ground to build a version of Tesla's gigafactory. The work inside is unlike anything autoworkers have ever done. Rather than repetitive work like swinging a dashboard inside a car and riveting the entire piece in place, battery cell workers will be minding robots and computers that handle chemical compounds.

When Ultium LLC opens the cell factory in 2022, the workers will run computers that controlled machines that mixed raw chemical materials into a slurry. That slurry becomes the thin wafers that go inside a sealed pouch that makes up a battery cell for GM vehicles.

I toured the plant in September of 2021. It was mostly a big box with battery cell–making equipment being installed. Instead of oiled-up assembly line equipment that would carry car bodies, the equipment looks more like a distillery with giant stainless vessels that will mix cell materials. It's really a chemical plant, said Ultium plant manager Tom Gallagher.

"There is no repetitive work activity for any employee in the plant," Gallagher said. "In manufacturing plants, people do repetitive work that is typically physically based. In our environment, there is none of that. I'm not hiring for physical competency. I'm hiring to be first responder on this line, which requires problem solving, critical thinking, making adjustments."

The new plant is very different from what people did on the assembly line for GM and their skills may not prepare them any better than someone who worked in retail, or administrative work, Gallagher said.

One of the challenges for GM and all carmakers as they race into the electric age is that nowhere in the world is there a labor force that is skilled and ready to make batteries, Gallagher said. Analytical skills and computer experience play far better with the hiring staff than lifting and bolting car parts on an assembly line.

What does that mean for laid-off GM workers in Lordstown?

"They need to apply and they will be considered like other candidates," Gallagher said. "We welcome their application. There is no preference to them as former GM employees or current GM employees. If they want to apply, they would need to leave General Motors because Ultium is an independent business."

The jobs don't pay as well, either. Ultium pays its production workers a base rate of $16 an hour and can go as high as $22. The job also offers a matching 401(k), healthcare starting on day one, and education reimbursement of up to $8,000 a year. All in all, Ultium's total compensation package is about $50,000 a year.

UAW workers start at $18.54 an hour and work their way up to $32.32. They also get big profit-sharing checks that exceeded $10,000 a year with the earnings GM was raking in. GM doesn't think that Ultium should pay that much because the prevailing wage in the battery industry is $17 or $18 an hour.

This is another way in which electrification puts the union in a tough spot. When GM closed Lordstown, it also shut down small transmission plants in Michigan and Maryland. In their place is the Ultium plant and another battery plant in Tennessee. Since Ultium is a GM-LG joint venture, it's not part of the master union agreement. So the UAW needs to have an organizing drive to get those workers to vote for union representation all over again.

The union would likely win in a place like Lordstown, but the UAW needs to go to the table and try to bargain for better pay and benefits. Dittes said the union will work to organize Lordstown. And he rejects the idea that those jobs should pay less, since, as Gallagher said, it's skilled work.

"In this conversion, Ford and GM will be making batteries here," Dittes said. "We have a lot of engine plants and transmission plants. Our members are worried about it. It's our job to make sure that all those pieces are made by our people."

If recent history is a guide, it could take the UAW years to get back to its top level of pay for battery workers. When the domestic auto industry was sailing into a crisis in 2007, the union agreed to a two-tiered wage. Starting workers got paid about $14.35 an hour and had no way to grow into the top pay of $32. Their pay maxed out at $19. They also did not have a pension or retiree healthcare like workers hired before the 2007 agreement.

Having workers make a different pay scale for the same work was anathema to unionism since the UAW's founding in 1935. Adjusted for inflation, that $14.35 starting wage was pretty close to the $5 a day that Henry Ford gave workers in 1914. In other words, the concessions made by the UAW in 2007 set the gains of collective bargaining back almost a century. And it took the UAW another eight years to get that pay back for all workers. Assuming the union organizes the GM and Ford battery plants, it could take the union the better part of a decade to get them the kind of pay that engine and transmission factory workers make now.

"It's really important that with all these offshoots and this new industry that we don't bring that standard of living down," Dittes said. "It will be our goal to keep that standard of living the same as it is for people making vehicles and engines."

That's what it's about for the union. Making sure the next generation of workers making electric vehicles has the same middle-class life as those who make cars today. But for former GM workers in Lordstown, it's either leave town or find a new gig.

Stav Diamandis had worked for GM for nineteen years when it closed. He didn't want to leave town and move his two high school kids. GM wanted him to build pickup trucks in Wentzville, Missouri. He took a pass and started painting houses. Eventually, he built the painting business into a company with five employees, and he makes more than he did at GM, but he has no healthcare or pension. He wouldn't work at the battery plant unless the pay and benefits were the same and he could start accumulating his pension benefits again.

"If the battery plant came calling, I'd have to listen to what they have to say," Diamandis said. "But if it's less than the $31 I made, no way. It would have to be coming back to my wage and benefits, with pension. I have one life to live. I'm going to live it the way I want to live it, not the way GM tells me to live it."

For Diamandis, GM's conversion to an electric future meant upheaval. But for a new kind of worker, it will be an opportunity, maybe even a homecoming. Ultium may not need traditional auto plant laborers, but it does create jobs for people with a different set of skills.

Ultium could end up being a draw for the region. GM is working with Youngstown State University to train workers and create the new workforce that can make battery cells. A team there developed an aptitude test for reading, math, and similar skills that will determine who gets into a training program. Those who do will be offered self-paced classes online before starting an on-the-job apprenticeship.

"Robots are doing all the hard work, and they just need problem solvers, critical thinkers, teamwork, collaboration," says Jennifer Oddo, who's overseeing the program at YSU.

There's something else, Oddo said. There aren't enough ready-made employees for Ultium in the region. The joint venture will likely have to cast a wider net to bring in people with the skills. If the Mahoning Valley becomes "Voltage Valley," people will be moving there.

Rana Abuhashim grew up in Macedonia, Ohio, near Lordstown. Her parents are Palestinian immigrants. She got a degree in chemical engineering from Youngstown State in 2019 and left for a job in Oklahoma with Goodyear Tire & Rubber.

When she read on LinkedIn that Ultium was hiring chemical engineers, she was intrigued. Abuhashim said she wanted to stay in the auto industry but was tired of making tires. She wanted to do something that made a difference. Being closer to family is also convenient. So she moved home and hired on to oversee mixing chemicals for the electrodes of the Ultium battery cells that will power GM's future electric vehicles.

"What's driving climate change is the pollution and what we're doing to the environment. Going to electrical will be a great starting point for the auto industry," she said. "Growing up, the Youngstown area has lacked job opportunities. By bringing in Ultium, it's bringing in green job opportunities to people."

⚡

CHAPTER 11

A DRIVERLESS FUTURE

The trouble with humans, one of them anyway, is that we do stupid things. Often. That's not so tragic if you forget your passport in a rush out the door to catch an early morning flight. Or, say, you get distracted by a text message and miss the only important thing said during a one-hour Zoom meeting at work. But when people rush around or lose focus while driving a 4,000-pound car on busy suburban streets at forty-five miles an hour, really bad things can happen.

Those kinds of mistakes end fatally at least 30,000 times a year in the US alone. That's one reason that universities, carmakers, and Silicon Valley tech companies began looking for ways to protect drivers from themselves and safeguard us from them. They figured if computers could fly planes on autopilot, why can't they drive cars?

The US military started pushing the idea of driverless cars back in 2004 with the Defense Advanced Research Projects Agency, or DARPA. The idea came from the military's desire to get vehicles to drive themselves so the Army and Marines could send machines into the most dangerous places in combat and protect soldiers. It would be especially useful to send robotically controlled supply trucks on roads that would likely have mines and explosive booby traps.

In what was called the "DARPA Challenge," fifteen teams were asked to come up with a self-driving vehicle that could run a 142-mile trek through the Mojave Desert. None of them finished. The best team created a vehicle that went a little more than seven miles, leaving the $1 million prize unclaimed. The next day, DARPA announced a second challenge for 2005.

This time it was a 132-mile course in southern Nevada. With more than a year to prepare, five of the 195 teams finished the course. Stanford University's team won the competition with a heavily modified autonomous Volkswagen Tuareg SUV named Stanley. The self-driving SUV made the desert haul in six hours and fifty-three minutes, bagging the $2 million prize. On the team were Sebastian Thrun and Andrei Aron, who would later be trailblazers in autonomous driving.

GM got hip to the idea after that. The company got involved in the 2007 DARPA Challenge. This one took it to the streets, by challenging the teams to complete a staged urban course in Victorville, California. Carnegie Mellon University teamed up with GM to wire up a self-driving Chevy Tahoe SUV. CMU's team was led by Chris Urmson, who would later become the technological brains behind Google's self-driving car program.

The teams competed over sixty miles on the George Air Force Base in California. They lost points for traffic violations and were rated on the time it took them to finish the event. There were moving obstacles placed on the course to simulate traffic, pedestrians, and many of the complexities that go along with city driving.

The Tahoe, which the researchers named "The Boss," won it for the CMU-GM team with an average speed of fourteen miles per hour and won $2 million. That led to forming a partnership that helped GM develop its own internal self-driving program. The timing was bad, though. It was late 2007 and the next year the nation and GM would be thrust into a financial crisis. There wasn't money or focus to develop self-driving technology.

Even though GM played the role of "Best Supporting Actor" in the pioneering effort, the team's bright stars, namely Urmson and Bryan Salesky, would later work for Google and take a leading role in developing autonomous technology. The next year, GM sank into a financial meltdown and was headed toward bankruptcy. Its self-driving car programs would be one of the last projects to get funding. The company was fighting for survival.

It's a shame, too, because the idea that cars could drive themselves—and save us from the drunks, the distracted, and the just plain inept—wasn't new. Like modern-era electric cars, autonomous driving was actually dusted off from the attic of once-great GM. The company had a presentation about self-driving cars at its 1939 World Fair Futurama expo.

In 1956, when Elvis Presley had topped the charts with "Don't Be Cruel" and "Hound Dog," GM showed off the Firebird III concept at its Motorama auto show. The car was part of the company's vision for a smart, interactive highway that had wires in the road that sent radio signals to the car to help it avoid accidents.[1]

It was primitive compared to the autonomous systems of today. Modern autonomy uses lidar, which sends out beams of laser light that read images up ahead and sends that data back to a computer, so the car can react. The cars also use radar and other sensors to read everything around it. And they have satellite-based mapping to know where to go.

With GM reeling from bankruptcy and going through a revolving door of CEOs in 2009, Google started working on self-driving cars. The company would have years of developing code, testing vehicles, and gathering data that other competitors didn't have.

When Barra took the job, the ignition crisis and troubled overseas operations occupied a lot of her time and was sucking up GM's cash. While she was mopping up messes from old GM, Google and Tesla were pressing ahead.

Those projects would send warning shots to Detroit in 2014, right around the time Barra was beginning to crawl out from under the ignition switch fiasco. In May, Google showed off its smiling two-seat pod that had been tooling around Mountain View, California, with a test driver in the front seat. The egg-shaped car could go no faster than about 25 mph, but it was on public roads and driving competently. Its hands-free driving was enabled by software that had learned the intricacies of avoiding people, dogs, and other vehicles, all while adhering to rules of the roads that its satellite mapping system laid out for it. The car wasn't ready for prime time, but it was a big step forward. Google spent six years testing the system over 1 million miles in Toyota and Lexus models, getting in just eleven accidents.[2]

Just a few months later, Tesla announced that all of its cars would be built with the hardware to support its Autopilot assisted driving system. Over the next two years, Musk planned to enable the hardware to work by sending car owners the Autopilot software over the air via satellite.

At the time, it wasn't clear how credible Musk's autonomy claims were. The company had survived longer than many investors and auto industry executives (many of whom privately wished Tesla would just go broke and go away) had even imagined. But Musk was famous for missing production dates and targets. His vehicles were constantly late, and he blew through deadlines like Congress during budget talks.

A year after Musk said his cars would be built with Auto-pilot hardware, Morgan Stanley's Adam Jonas nearly doubled his price target for Tesla to $465 from $280. The shares were trading at $243 the day the report came out.

Jonas's logic: Tesla would be launching an app-based, on-demand mobility service. He writes that he could envision "Tesla Mobility, an app-based, on-demand mobility service." He reckoned that Tesla's self-driving hardware would eventually be enabled by software. When it was, owners could drive the car to work and then release it to a network of shared vehicles that others would rent out by the hour like a Zipcar vehicle or by the day like Airbnb.

It would be transportation's version of Jack Lemmon's pad in *The Apartment*. People only used their cars 4 percent of the time on average, Jonas reckoned. They'd offer to rent it out the rest of the time and Tesla could cash in on providing the service.

"Tesla is uniquely positioned, in our view, to solve the biggest flaw in the auto industry, less than 4% utilization, via an app-based, on-demand mobility service," he wrote.

Jonas was convinced Tesla had the technology and ability to hire talent that would make it a leader. There were a few problems: the service didn't exist, Tesla hadn't talked about it, and Autopilot was not fully autonomous.

There were also flaws with that business model. People own lots of things that they don't use very often, but they don't all want to loan out their goods. Sure, some people rent out their homes through Airbnb but most do not.

Be that as it may, Google and Tesla had self-driving systems that were starting to hatch. GM and its venerable peers did not. They were all working on advanced safety systems that could help drivers avoid accidents and trying to get them to drive cars on their own, but real self-drive was a long way off.

Google talked about safety a lot, but in reality, Wall Street and Silicon Valley saw billions to be mined from cars that could drive themselves. Uber's fast-growing driving service turned over about 80 percent of its billings to the driver. They didn't pay them very much, but they knew that if they could get the human out, the business was potentially very profitable.

Plus, Google already had people glued to their PCs and smartphones all day and evening. The one hour they didn't have (besides sleep) was the thirty minutes to and from work that people were driving. That would give their advertising clients a whole new dimension. They could reach people while they were in the car if only their eyes weren't on the road. Google could use that driving data to direct people to car washes, gas stations, hotels, restaurants, anything. It was a growth machine.

The data collected from how people drive, where they go, and when would be of immense value to insurance companies. Insurers would give lower rates to safe drivers and penalize unsafe motorists. Retailers could reach out to people as they passed by. Dealers and repair shops could preempt mechanical and electrical problems and offer services.

With all of these ideas to make money from autonomy, Wall Street was pouring money into electric-vehicle and autonomous startups. Tesla was a darling and Google had yet another way to find growth. At that point, no one thought that the likes of GM, Ford, Toyota, or Volkswagen would solve the most difficult challenge of our time. The prevailing narrative said that Detroit's carmakers were dinosaurs and Big Tech would bring their extinction.

There would be another worrying development for GM. Google had hired former Hyundai North America CEO John Krafcik to run the driverless project. That was the strongest indicator yet that Google was looking for ways to build a business with self-driving cars and that it could beat carmakers with a self-driving service.

Krafcik was the real deal. He had run Hyundai's US business for five years, ending in 2013. On his watch, the Korean automaker had built North American plants and almost doubled US sales to 760,000 vehicles annually. Before that, he was in product development at Ford, where he got the Expedition and Lincoln Navigator SUVs into production. He understood manufacturing very well. That gave Google the combination of an army of code writers and an auto industry insider who could commercialize the business. The company also had $73 billion in cash and a tremendous ability to hire talent. They just didn't have a car of their own.

Tesla did and Autopilot also beat GM to market. The system enables the car to steer and brake for the driver, but they needed to keep eyes on the road and engage as the car was headed to an off ramp. Musk would later catch heat from regulators for calling it Autopilot, when in fact it still required the driver to pay attention.

With self-driving cars, GM and its traditional rivals were all playing catch-up. And they had to. If someone could get it to work, it would be the pinnacle of automotive safety. It could also change the way people buy transportation. How Barra handled the transition to autonomous driving would determine GM's success for years into the future.

It was another race where GM was trying to catch up. She had a mission to be part of, if not jump to the head of the pack in, the technological transformation of the industry. She reckoned that electrification was here to stay and autonomous cars were closer to reality. Ridesharing and connected cars were other services changing transportation.

Barry Engle, a former Ford Brasil (the Brazilian subsidiary of the Ford Motor Company) executive who was working at a clean-energy startup, talked to Barra at the time. She was trying to recruit him to run GM's South American business. As part of the job, he would also be on her twelve-member Senior Leadership Team that would decide the company's strategy in key areas, especially new technology.

"She was able to articulate for me this vision she had for the company and how those trends were real and she was determined to be at the forefront," Engle said. "I hadn't heard a CEO be so passionate about it. She talked about the disruption of the industry and how she wanted to control it and lead it and control our own destiny rather than trailing behind."

Engle decided to join. He admired Barra's vision and also saw that the company had a self-driving car program and had worked on electric vehicles since the 1990s. GM may have been fixing itself, but the company had some strengths, Engle said.

In 2015, Barra took her management team on a field trip to Silicon Valley. They went to Stanford and met up with start-ups and Big Tech companies. She wanted the team to see what they were up against and also soak up the entrepreneurial spirit that the valley had.

"My view was, there's disruption coming," Barra told me. "We have to either lead transformation or sit back and be disrupted. That really wasn't even an option. We need to put the might of General Motors behind this."

There was one big problem. GM was behind in development. The company's autonomous work was focused on developing Super Cruise, which was similar to Tesla's Autopilot except that it was intended to let drivers go hands-free on the highway. They would have to remain engaged in case the vehicle got in a sticky situation or went back to suburban roads. It helped keep drivers out of accidents and let them relax while cruising on the highway, but neither system was truly driverless.

The idea with Super Cruise was to take existing technologies like adaptive cruise control, which maintained a car's speed on the highway but slowed it down if it started bearing down on another car's rear end, with another system that follows digitally mapped roads and keeps a car in its lane if the driver veers to either side. If GM could make those systems work and enhance them, the company could keep improving it until the car could eventually master self-driving.

In the early days, it wasn't going so well. GM was testing cars at its Tech Center in Warren, Michigan, and its huge proving ground in Milford, a scenic hamlet west of Detroit where the automaker has a 4,000-acre test site to try out future models without having to worry about prying eyes, pedestrians, other drivers, or the cops.

The self-driving pilot vehicles rarely left those sites. The engineers wanted to keep them in the cocoon because they could only handle basic driving and topped out at twenty-five miles per hour. There were some pretty basic things that GM's car couldn't do, according to Doug Parks.[3] The cars had trouble with left turns if other cars were coming. They also were flummoxed by parked cars on the side of the road. They had a tough time swerving around them, he said.

Even in 2015, when Google was publicly showing its cars on public roads, GM was still trying to master some basic driving situations. That summer, Reuss took *BusinessWeek* writer Keith Naughton on a test drive. They were in a Cadillac CT6, which is the big sedan that GM used to pilot the system. A test car blew by the Caddy to the left and another slowed down on the right side. Confused, Super Cruise disengaged. A crescent-shaped light on the steering wheel went from green to red and the system disengaged. Reuss had to take over.

At the time, one senior GM engineer lamented to me that he had scores of engineers who could tinker with brake calipers and exhaust systems, but far too few who could write code. GM simply needed more expertise if Barra wanted to be a true player in autonomous driving.

"We knew we didn't have it because it was never designed to do it," Reuss told me in an interview. "At the time, it was, 'my gosh, we're just not there.'"

To the company's credit, GM had been looking for technology among self-driving startups. It started its own venture capital fund called GM Ventures under Whitacre in 2010. Alisyn Malek, who had a job scouting ideas for GM Ventures, had been looking for a startup with skills in the kind of mapping needed for autonomous driving and vehicle navigation.

She stumbled onto Cruise Automation, a startup founded by video game entrepreneur Kyle Vogt, who made a fortune cofounding and selling Twitch, an app that enables video gamers to gather and watch others play. It also enabled people to create their own shared entertainment content online. Amazon bought Twitch for $970 million in 2014, so Vogt took his share of the spoils and started working with self-driving car software. The MIT graduate had worked on the 2004 DARPA Challenge and always had a passion for cars.

Cruise Automation had been working with software and a lidar-based hardware system that was rigged into Vogt's Audi A4 sedan. The car was driving around San Francisco for testing. With its steep cobblestone streets and labyrinthian layout, the Golden Gate City is the most brutal environment for self-driving software, not to mention for human drivers. If self-driving software can make it there, it could probably make it in New York, too. Suburban streets and highways would be a snap. Vogt's people were certainly ahead of GM's.

Vogt's plan was to develop a system that people could buy and retrofit into their cars. That way they didn't have to wait for future models. Their existing vehicle could be made to drive on its own. The business plan would have serious hurdles with auto safety regulations. Getting approval for something like that takes a lot of time, testing, money, and attorneys. But Vogt did have the beginnings of a system that was already doing more than GM could do.

"We went on the lookout," Reuss said. "Dan Ammann and myself and Doug Parks, we started looking at different ways to do it. We visited [Google] and a bunch of things on the West Coast. Cruise, we went and looked deeply at what they were doing."

Ultimately, said Malek, "the tech team saw that Cruise could move more quickly than GM could."

Barra thought GM should buy the company and Ammann's team started negotiating a deal. In doing so, they tore a page from Procter & Gamble CEO A.G. Lafley's strategy on innovation. Lafley believed that it was acceptable and even necessary to look outside of his own walls to find something ground-breaking. He liked to pair up R&D with an innovation model called Connect & Develop, or C&D. If you found a good idea, even with a competitor, pair up and get it to market. Working alone, he reckoned, growth would come too slowly.

GM courted Cruise by dangling $1.15 billion and by showing Vogt that he could use the company's Bolt electric car to work on the technology. Self-driving cars use a lot of computing power. Having a massive battery on board would power it all easily. Since GM had a factory that could churn out as many cars as Vogt needed—and had engineers to integrate the software and hardware into the cars—he could have an advantage that even Google lacked.

When GM bought Cruise in early 2016, the automaker instantly got itself into the race. Cruise wasn't as far along as Google in terms of development, but its cars were moving about San Francisco and learning via artificial intelligence how to better navigate urban driving. The idea was to pair the startup's software brains with GM's knowledge of the car and make integration of robotic driving more seamless. When the technology was ready, GM could just start building them.

It was a big advantage over Google, Reuss said. GM and its autonomous technology partner were joined at the hip. While Google would have to cut deals with automakers to get cars and then work to integrate its system into them, GM and Cruise could get the technology into the cars while they were testing the system.

It all sounded good, but there was still huge risk for Barra. What if she picked the wrong company? There were other startups out there and the technology was so difficult to perfect that it was tough to assess which players were really competent. By acquiring Cruise, GM would have to spend billions to help the company develop self-driving technology.

Ammann figured that, since self-driving systems were so expensive and difficult to develop, there would be a big shakeout. Eventually, the field would be winnowed down to a handful of companies that offered a suite of autonomous hardware and software the same way the smartphone world had gotten down to two major operating systems, Google's Android and Apple iOS.

Suppose GM plowed billions into developing its own self-driving system, only to be outspent and outsmarted by Google, Apple, Tesla, Amazon, or one of the startups? It was a calculated risk that Barra was willing to take, but one she needed to make to get in the race.

With Kyle Vogt reporting to Ammann, Cruise was in a race to catch up to Google (which had named its self-driving unit Waymo) and hopefully beat the well-funded giant at providing a robotic competitor to Uber. To prove Cruise could do it, GM invited media and Wall Street analysts to San Francisco in November 2017. They had rides in the car with a safety driver, which the company didn't know was not allowed per state rules in California.

When I got into the car, the first thing I noticed was how incredibly slow the drive was. The idea, Vogt told me, was safety, not excitement. The car came up behind a garbage truck. It wasn't moving and neither was Cruise's Bolt AV for a few awkward moments. With its lidar and sensors surveying the scene ahead and showing a clear passing lane on a computer screen on the dashboard, it finally skulked past the garbage hauler.

The car was even more ponderous when we pulled up behind a food truck. Ten seconds went by and nothing. The car's artificial eyes detected an oncoming car and waited another five seconds. Finally, after waiting twenty-six seconds in all, it crawled past the truck.

Later in the ride, we entered a roundabout. In Europe, where roundabouts are de rigueur, people blast through so long as no cars are coming. The Bolt AV entered the roundabout and stopped. It pumped the brakes a couple of times before finally heading through. There had been no cars to avoid.

Cruise's system didn't really do anything wrong. It was just slow and boring to ride, at its best, and ponderous and sloppy at its worst. And that's the point Vogt told me afterward.

"Comfort and smoothness of ride is a distant priority after making the vehicle safe," Vogt said. "Over the company's three-year history, only about 2 percent of the time have we considered any element of smoothness or comfort. It has been entirely about getting you there safely."[4]

Despite the slow and occasionally herky-jerky ride, Cruise was determined to be on the road. The company planned to have a fleet of cars in service by the end of 2019. GM and Cruise had some grandiose plans on the kind of revenue they would be raking in.

Ammann said that GM's plan was to get self-driving cars to market in large numbers, which would enable the company to drop the costs of ridesharing to less than $1 a mile by 2025. Uber and Lyft were charging $2 to $3 a mile with a human driver at the wheel. Once Cruise gets the cost that low, GM estimated that 75 percent of the miles people need to travel could be through a sharing or hailing service. He saw a $1.6 trillion market.

"It's a big opportunity," said Ammann at the time. "We think it will change the world."

While Ammann was in San Francisco mapping out GM's self-driven road to riches, Waymo had plans to use Chrysler minivans to start piloting a self-driving ride-hailing business and was working on a plan to buy 20,000 Jaguar I-Pace electric SUVs and 60,000 Chrysler Pacifica minivans that would be fitted up to drive themselves. Uber planned to use as many as 24,000 Volvo SUVs for the same purpose. Tesla was also developing its hands-free Full-Self Driving system.

Ammann also had a plan to defray the cost. GM budgeted $1 billion a year. That was a big sum for a company that also had to develop an entire lineup of electric vehicles. And it might not be enough. The former investment banker went out to find multiple partners to help fund and foster development.

He first brought in Japanese investment giant SoftBank Vision Fund in May 2018, which had invested in several good delivery startups that would benefit from self-driving vehicles. The company pledged to put in $2.25 billion over time, if Cruise hit certain development milestones. In October, Honda

Motor Company agreed to put in $750 million for a stake plus spend another $2 billion over twelve years as Cruise developed the system.

Barra made a key decision at that point. She knew that taking Cruise from a startup to a real business would require someone with business management chops. The company would also have to raise cash. With Ammann's experience as president of GM and his investment banking connections, he would be the one to do it.

She sent him to San Francisco to do just that in January 2019. A few months later, he had brought in yet another investor. Money manager T. Rowe Price Associates Inc. put in $1.15 billion, which gave Cruise an implied value of $19 billion. With Ammann running the company, he and Barra were beginning to pull off the improbable feat of convincing investors that a 120-year-old car company could be a player in a software-based competition of getting cars to drive themselves.

Accolades are great. So is investor interest. Now comes the hard part: getting the cars to drive themselves. Throughout that summer, Cruise was driving its heavily modified Chevy Bolt autonomous electric cars around several planned routes in San Francisco. The company was constantly reducing the number of times the test driver had to take the wheel, which are called "disengagements" in the geeky world of self-drive engineering.

It's an imprecise measurement because one driver may be more nervous than another when testing an autonomous car and disengage the autonomous system more often. Be that as it may, Cruise test drivers had to grab the wheel once every 12,000 miles. Waymo drivers had to do it every 13,000 miles, according to data from the California Department of Motor Vehicles. No other AV company was close to Cruise and Waymo.

Even with progress being made, Ammann had reservations about starting a service before the end of the year. Before he arrived, the plan was to run a service in an easily navigated area like South San Francisco, Palo Alto, or Phoenix, where Waymo was running its pilot service.

That would be the easy route. Suburban streets are straight and wide. There can be heavy traffic, but they have simple turns, few pets and pedestrians, and no delivery trucks clogging up tight city streets. The car basically has to follow traffic rules and stop if someone jumps out into a crosswalk.

Cruise could run a simple service in Phoenix and stage a glitzy press event, but Ammann didn't think it would accomplish much. If the cars still couldn't navigate the labyrinthian and often chaotic streets of places like New York and San Francisco, then it defeated the purpose of autonomous cars. The whole idea was to replace personal transport and all the congestion and parking woes that it brings with a shared ride. And while doing so, GM would tap into revenue from an urban consumer whom the company never sees.

Throughout spring, Ammann was watching to see if it looked like Cruise would be able to have cars ready and if the company would even be able to get regulatory approvals to do so. When achieving both looked more remote, he realized the company wouldn't hit its goal. Barra, too, became less and less committed to the 2019 goal in her public statements.

At the company's annual meeting in June, she wouldn't be drawn into confirming a 2019 launch for a service. Still, in her public appearances, Barra's posture about having a service ready by the end of 2019 had gone from confident to noncommittal. At the company's annual meeting in June, she passed on a chance to say that the company's plan was on schedule. She said instead that GM had to hit certain safety and validation milestones.

"As we achieve those milestones, we will then be in a position in a geofenced environment to truly launch an AV system without a driver," she said. "So we'll be gated by safety."

Cruise wasn't ready. Ammann wrote a blog post on Cruise's website saying the company wouldn't hit its target. It must have been a bitter pill to swallow. The post described the process Cruise would put in place to safely deploy its autonomous cars, and how the self-driving EVs would be better for the city's emissions and safer for its thoroughfares.

At about the fifteenth paragraph, Ammann finally said GM wouldn't hit its target to start a service by the end of the year.

"When you're working on the large-scale deployment of mission critical safety systems, the mindset of 'move fast and break things' certainly doesn't cut it," he wrote. "With such high stakes, our first deployment needs to be done right and we will only deploy when we can demonstrate that we will have a net positive impact on safety on our roads."

In an interview after, Ammann refused to give a timeline to start the business. He wasn't alone as the entire self-driving world was taking a big time-out. Waymo, too, had fallen short of its goal. The Google unit had planned to be the first to start a driverless ride-hailing service before the end of 2018, but only made the service available to a limited number of residents in suburban Phoenix; and it kept safety drivers in its minivans. The company also planned to have a fleet giving 1 million rides a day by late 2019, according to the *New York Times*, but missed that goal.

There were serious reasons for caution. An Uber Technologies Inc. test vehicle killed a pedestrian who was walking across the road in Arizona in March 2018, which set off a firestorm of questions over the safety of self-driving cars. By the time Ammann called a halt on Cruise's plans, three

Tesla drivers had died on US roads while using its Autopilot system.

Waymo reined its plans in. While the company did start offering truly driverless rides in Arizona, it also backed off its initially aggressive plans. In 2017, the company planned to be offering services in nine cities in eighteen months. It didn't happen, Bloomberg reported. And the tens of thousands of Jaguar SUVs and Chrysler minivans? They weren't ordered in big numbers even by late 2021.[5]

All of this is to say that getting robots to replace drivers—that revolutionary idea that Ammann called this generation's "moon shot"—is actually harder than getting to the moon. Scientists licked that challenge in 1969. Mars shot might be more accurate.

While Vogt and his code writers kept working to get the engineering down, Ammann kept building a business. In January 2021, the company showed off the Origin, a self-driving shuttle that seats four and could be configured to hold six. It had no steering wheel or pedals. This was a true AV designed to pick up a handful of people and take them wherever they want to go. On the outside, it's a breadbox with sensors and lidar built into the top corners and other spaces in the body panels. Inside, two rows of seats face each other with no cockpit.

The Origin is the ultimate expression of Barra's "zero, zero, zero" pledge. It's electric and emission free. It drives itself, thus avoiding accidents. And with space for up to six people, it could be shared and cut down congestion. The Origin runs on the same battery and electric motor that powers GM's Hummer EV, the electric Silverado pickup, and all of the trucks and SUVs that will be built in the Detroit-Hamtramck plant. That combined Cruise's software talent with GM's ability to mass-produce vehicles. It's the combination that Barra

ADRIVERLESSFUTURE

said would give Cruise and GM a big advantage over startups and even Waymo.

Ammann kept up fundraising too. In early 2021, he convinced software giant Microsoft to lead a new funding round of $2 billion. Microsoft had expertise in cloud computing, which would help GM run networks of self-driving vehicles that commuters could summon just as they would a car from Uber or Lyft. The cash infusion was estimated to have a value of $30 billion. GM's stock ran up almost 10 percent that day. Cruise now really did have investors convinced that it could be a leader.

As the year progressed, Ammann and Vogt were getting more comfortable with the technology and were getting ready to put paying customers from the buying public in Cruise's cars. They applied for permits to start charging for rides in San Francisco and had a plan to scale up a massive business. Barring any unforeseen problems, Cruise was on the verge of launching an automated rival to Uber and Lyft.

Those two companies lose money. GM figures that removing the driver with autonomous technology is the only way to make the business profitable.

CHAPTER 12

⚡

CHARGING AHEAD

Barra joined Mark Reuss, Doug Parks, and one of her top engineers, Josh Tavel, in Reuss's office in downtown Detroit in March 2019. The company had announced what was at the time an aggressive EV plan months earlier. They had a battery pack in the works with Korea's LG Chem. That pack would serve as the foundation for a variety of EVs. The question now was which vehicle should come to market first and how soon.

GM already had the Chevy Bolt on sale and plans for a slightly larger version of that car, called a Bolt EUV. Those were small and relatively inexpensive EVs. It was a practical choice for the kind of buyer who couldn't afford the Tesla Model 3, which started at more than $40,000 but typically sold for much more. But there was nothing breakthrough about the Bolt duo. They used GM's second-generation battery and couldn't get the minimum 300 miles of range offered by Tesla's models.

Everyone was trailing Tesla and racing to catch up. GM needed to get its plans rolling fast. The company needed something breakthrough, too. Something totally different. The Bolt had been a decent start, but Ultium would be its big play.

Reuss had an idea. What if GM brought back the Hummer brand and developed an electric pickup that did everything a truck could, but without the gas-hog emissions? His idea was that a battery-powered Hummer would turn on its head what many consumers thought of electric vehicles. Despite Tesla's success, many car buyers still viewed EVs as a science project. They saw plug-ins as small cars or midsized sedans, and expensive. Many people didn't think cars could go far on a single charge. Even a Model 3 with the longer-range battery could only go 310 miles on a charge. Gasoline-powered vehicles went much farther on a full tank. Plus, Americans love big SUVs and pickups, and no none was selling either with battery power.

An electric Hummer would be big, powerful, and have the ability to tow, haul, and go off road. It was the exact opposite of everything that green cars had been since Toyota and Honda started the hybrid craze in the late '90s with the tiny Insight two-seater and compact Prius.

A zero-emission Hummer would also be a turnabout for the name. When GM acquired the brand in 1999 and built the H2, it got about ten miles to the gallon and became a lightning rod for environmentalists. The Sierra Club launched an entire ad campaign lampooning the car as yesteryear's technology. They created a website called "HummerDinger" to mock the SUV. "G.M. celebrates Hummer's state-of-the-art 1950's engine technology with some of today's hottest stars, naming Pat Boone and Frankie Avalon as pitchmen."[1]

GM wound the brand down in 2010. Sales slumped amid higher gasoline prices and increased consumer sensitivity to climate change. Reuss's idea would change the image of EVs and Hummer. And, as Tavel put it, he and his team would be doing "epic shit."

Barra loved the idea. She turned to Tavel and asked how quickly his team could get it ready for market. He responded that the usual four- or five-year development time for new vehicles would be needed. That meant 2023 at best.

"She said fourth quarter of '21. I said, 'I know you're thinking that but this is a five-year development timing,'" Tavel said. "I said something somewhere in the middle. She said, 'I think it needs to be Q4 of '21.'"

Then Parks chimed in to buy the team more time. Barra was insistent and the engineers agreed, even though they had no idea how he and his crew would get it done. Tavel did have one stipulation.

I said, "I build my team and you guys stay out of my way."

The next day, he and Parks sat down and put together a dedicated project team. They would rely on virtual engineering tools and a streamlined approval process. The Ultium battery's so-called skateboard architecture makes up the base of a car that allows automakers to develop new vehicles with fewer scale models fashioned out of clay or steel parts. Heavy use of computer engineering cuts the budget for prototype cars and parts compared with physical models.

This was another key moment for GM. The thinking previously was it would take longer for truck buyers to go electric than your typical suburban SUV buyer. GM had been working on a deal with Rivian Automotive to use the EV startup's truck battery and platform and jointly develop trucks for GM. Early in 2019, it looked like a deal was in hand that would give GM exclusive use of Rivian's platform for seven years, while Rivian also developed its own truck and SUV. But the deal was falling apart.

Rivian founder R.J. Scaringe was leery of giving GM exclusivity, but he knew the automaker's industrial might could help him get manufacturing going.[2] Still, his business plan had rested in part on selling the platform to other companies. Rivian would make its own vehicles, develop others for shareholder Amazon.com Inc., and sell the platform to other carmakers. Scaringe was also worried that the GM deal would command too much of Rivian's resources. While GM was working on the deal, rival Ford made a surreptitious pass at Rivian with its then-president, Joe Hinrichs, giving Scaringe an out, according to the *Wall Street Journal*.[3] GM's old foe offered a deal to invest $500 million in the company, jointly develop an electric truck, and let Rivian do whatever it wants with its technology and with whomever. It was a deal that was very favorable to Rivian, said one person close to the discussions.

When Rivian walked away from GM, Reuss was perturbed, say people close to him. The company quickly moved to adapt Ultium for trucks. Reuss also wanted an electric Hummer to start GM's plug-in pickup business and with the nice side benefit that it would take on Rivian's R1T electric pickup in the nascent EV truck market. But GM would have to work fast.

Tavel set up a team to do it. He detonated the meeting culture that could make vehicle development such a ponderous process. To get around the typically hours-long and overstaffed committee meetings at GM's tech center campus north of Detroit, Tavel held an open meeting every day at noon with a one-hour time limit for team members gathered around a wooden table. There was no agenda. If someone had an issue, they could show up. If not, they had no obligation to be there. He borrowed Amazon.com Inc.'s two-pizza rule to keep delays to a minimum.

"If you can't feed everyone there with two pizzas, you have too many people there," Tavel says.

He wanted quick solutions to the kinds of issues that come up in car making. Early on, designers had planned to give the Hummer removable roof panels for open-air driving. Tavel's plan was to put the four removable panels in the front trunk, or frunk, as Tesla's cars have. That would mean horse trading for space with other engineers who were using space for other parts of the vehicle. The engineer working on the roof panels prepared a PowerPoint deck to show the options.[4]

Tavel, who grew up with a wrench in his hand and raced cars as a kid, told the engineer that they didn't have time for the usual corporate fandango. He just told him to make a decision and inform the team. If anyone had an issue, they could come to the noon meeting, which was really just an open forum, and have it out. There weren't major objections and the project trundled on. Debate averted.

The Hummer team had a policy of making all decisions within twenty-four hours so small issues wouldn't balloon into a major delay. When Barra would call him to check on progress, her questions were mostly about timing and whether he needed any help navigating the vastness of GM, Tavel said. Barra told him that she wanted the Hummer team and its speed to market to serve as a flag bearer for what was possible.

The truck itself is a behemoth. It weighs more than 9,000 pounds, has the equivalent of 1,000 horsepower, and can go from zero to sixty in three seconds. With its price range of $80,000 to $110,000, it will sell in relatively small numbers. But it could make money at that price and also give GM a start on the pickup truck platform that would be a base for Chevy Silverado pickup and Cadillac Escalade that run on electric power. One problem: it's too heavy for most driveways.

For GM, this was about creating buzz for electric trucks and galvanizing the engineers internally to do something car guys think is cool—and get it done at what Barra calls "ventilator speed." GM got the Hummer done in thirty months from the time of the meeting in Reuss's office. Once they had a truck built on the Ultium platform, making a Chevy Silverado pickup was easier, Tavel said. The truck team had already built a pickup truck using the battery pack and motors. They would just have to make one that's more practical.

The collapse of the Rivan deal didn't cost GM much in terms of time to market. Parks and his team started working on a truck version of the battery pack and were ready to start the Hummer and Silverado quickly. But GM did miss out on a massive payday after Rivian's highly successful stock offering. Ford's $500 million investment in the company in 2019 earned it an 11 percent stake that would be worth more than $2 billion even as Rivian shares tumbled early in 2022.

With the Hummer well underway, Tavel's group started on the Silverado. That, too, would be a sprint. While GM was developing the Hummer, Ford announced that it would sell an electric version of its popular F-150 pickup by May 2022. That would be almost a year ahead of GM's timing. Rivian was also moving quickly on its R1T pickup truck, and Tesla had its Cybertruck in the works.

GM's Hummer truck would beat all competitors to market, albeit as a hulking off-road curio. Its rapid development resulted in a truck battery and platform that Tavel and his team could use to quickly prepare the Silverado-E. GM was scheduled to arrive months later than both its old enemy Ford and its new rival Rivian. But with a dedicated truck platform, Chevy would likely be able to offer more driving miles on a full charge than either one, Tavel said.

When reflecting on GM's race to develop its electric trucks, the long hours for his team, and the nights he fell asleep on the couch with his laptop on his chest, Tavel commends Barra for pushing so hard.

"Can you imagine if Mary had listened to me?" Tavel said. "What a disaster that would have been. Fortunately, we're there. Rivian would have been there first. The F150, it'll be a good truck, but they have 300 miles of range. We'll have 400 miles. Mary is the one that set the vision."

Barra had good reasons to push. GM saw increasing interest from consumers in its own internal research. She saw an inflection point coming and was racing to get out in front of it. Throughout 2019, EV sales were growing. They were only 2.5 percent of the US market, but they had grown from tens of thousands a year to more than 300,000 by late 2020. GM also saw that its competitors were going to get electric pickups to market first and the company had to protect one of its best markets.

In states that had zero-emission vehicle regulations and mandates, EVs made up about 5 percent of the market, according to the think tank International Council on Clean Transportation. Those are coastal areas like New York, California, New England, and the Pacific Northwest. That is to say, places where domestic brands fare poorly and affluent consumers have greater interest in having the latest technologies.

It was also clear that electric trucks would have serious demand. Sure, maybe farmers in rural states would take longer to convince and it might be years before charging infrastructure made its way to the prairie, but commercial users would like the lower energy and repair costs. Companies that needed fleets of vans and pickups also wanted to gain green bragging rights as companies faced more pressure to show progress on environmental, social, and governance issues. ESG, as it was called, was becoming a hot topic. Companies are under heavy pressure to show that they are reducing their carbon footprint and promoting diversity in their ranks. EVs will help with the carbon requirements.

Investors saw the growth, too. EV sales were small but growing, while the overall vehicle market had been flat or down slightly. That means all the growth for carmakers is in EVs. Tesla's market cap started 2019 at just above $50 billion and passed GM to end the year at $80 billion. Its value soared to close to $700 billion by the end of 2020. Startups were luring investment capital, too. Amazon invested $700 million in Rivian in 2019 and even more in 2020. By the end of 2021, Rivian's total stock value would be higher than $90 billion, about $5 billion more than GM.

The political climate also changed to favor electric drive. Joe Biden had defeated Donald Trump in November 2020. After a week of recounts, lawsuits, and conspiracy theories, Biden declared victory as president-elect on November 10. In his infrastructure plan, he pledged to push electric vehicles with a proposal to replenish funding for EV tax credits for consumers and to build charging stations across the US.

Just nine days later after Biden declared victory, Barra plowed more money into GM's EV play. She dedicated another $7 billion to a budget that was already $20 billion and expanded the planned lineup by ten more vehicles. She declared that some, like the Cadillac Lyriq SUV, would be for sale sooner than originally planned. Barra also said that there would be mass-market EVs that would sell for less than $35,000, which is the heart of the new-vehicle market in the US.[5]

It would take some courage to stick to the spending plan. While GM was boosting its EV investments, a crisis in semiconductor supply was starting to bubble up. The Trump administration had put China's Semiconductor Manufacturing International Corp. on a blacklist of companies with ties to the Chinese military, which meant US makers of key software needed by the chipmaker couldn't sell to the company without a license.[6] The move hurt the Chinese company's ability to make the most advanced chips, which sent some of its customers to producers in Taiwan and Korea that were already maxed out.[7]

At the same time, sales of consumer electronics were soaring, which put heavy demand on the chip industry. Frequent shutdowns at semiconductor plants due to the Covid-19 pandemic further exacerbated the shortage. Then, a fire at a plant owned by Japanese semiconductor producer Renesas hit the supply chain hard.[8]

Like consumer electronics makers, car companies were putting ever more electronics and connected services like navigation in their cars. That meant more and more semiconductors. In 2005, the auto industry bought about $16 billion in chips. By 2020, that grew to more than $40 billion, according to McKinsey.

GM saw the shortage coming in late 2020 and started stocking up on chips, but no automaker would be immune. Consulting firm Alix Partners forecasted that the industry would lose 3.9 million vehicles' worth of production in 2021 and later upped that to 7.7 million vehicles. Taken together, the auto industry would lose $210 billion in revenue off a base of $3.5 trillion.

Barra faced a choice of whether or not to take a time-out and halt some vehicle programs until the company could get more clarity into the semiconductor problem and how it might hit production, and hence cash flow. She decided to continue pushing, said GM's newly minted chief financial officer, Paul Jacobson, who was hired in December 2020 after leaving Delta Air Lines.

Not only was Barra keeping investment intact, but in January she made an announcement that would resonate beyond her overworked engineers and eager shareholders: GM would be carbon neutral by 2035. That meant that GM wouldn't sell vehicles that burned any fossil fuels after that time. GM's stock ran up more than 3 percent that day.

The *New York Times* captured the moment saying that "the days of the internal combustion engine are numbered."[9]

The proclamation was an embrace of calls from the Democrats to curb climate change. It mirrored California governor Gavin Newsome's executive order banning the sale of gasoline-burning vehicles in the state by 2035.

Still, the plan wasn't just about politics, playing nice with the new administration in Washington, or global warming. Barra is betting the house that EVs will bring in new buyers. After downsizing for decades, including the first three years of her own tenure as CEO, Barra was going on the offensive.

The company started building a ten-year growth plan in February. Barra decided to split GM's annual budget process from its long-term budgeting plan, Jacobson said. Instead of having finance come up with the long-term plan, every business leader in GM had to come up with their own strategic direction and growth targets along with it. From there, Jacobson said, Barra's team would look at the capital requirements for each unit and pull a cohesive plan together.

It involved every corner of GM. Reuss's new products and growth plans in the core automotive business were the centerpiece. But with it came plans to grow GM's BrightDrop electric delivery van unit by selling to fleet customers like UPS, FedEx, perhaps Amazon, and any small business that needed vans. Ammann's aspirations for Cruise's self-driving car services would play a big role. So would a plan to grow revenue by selling software-based services, which included map-based applications and subscriptions to GM's Super Cruise hands-free driving system that operated on Cadillac models. There would also be a push to sell insurance policies and get more out of lending arm GM Financial.

The first piece would be another acceleration of the electric-vehicle plans. In June, GM added $8 billion to its EV bet. Within that spending, GM would accelerate plans to build EVs and some of the battery plants, Jacobson said.

In total, Barra had now committed $35 billion with a plan to build thirty electric vehicles globally and four US battery plants by 2025. When reflecting on the company's rapid acceleration of EV spending and launch plans, Barra said it was a growing understanding of where the world was headed along with a confidence that GM could develop vehicles that address consumer resistance to plug-in cars, trucks, and SUVs.

"We were looking at consumer and customer research to understand what we needed to solve to win them over," Barra said. "I'd rather drive EV adoption from a customer desire perspective than a regulatory perspective. We were identifying what their concerns and challenges are. There is much more willingness to consider EV now than there was even two years ago."

Barra said GM had been looking at the growth of regulations in China and Europe, too, and realizing there was no going back. But more and more, studies showed that consumers were ready to embrace the change to electric drive. Consideration among car buyers for EVs as their next purchase was rising rapidly. She said GM was also getting battery costs down and driving range up. That led to increasing confidence that, if GM made great EVs, buyers would be there.

"There wasn't this data that we put our finger on and said, 'This proves it,'" she said. "It was, 'Let's go.' It was a belief in where the world was heading and seizing that. You need to know both, but every now and then you need to make the call."

By the spring of 2021, GM had more fear of missing out than worry that buyers won't show up. Jacobson said that the moves made that year were about making sure GM had the production available to meet demand.

"One of the things we've talked about internally is that, if we build a battery plant that sits idle for three years because of a slowdown in EV adoption, I'd rather make that mistake than build a battery plant as quickly as we can because we're behind the curve," Jacobson said. "We can't afford to miss late on these things."

The bigger risk was that GM waited too long and other competitors had electric versions of big-volume market segments where GM had a big position—like midsized SUVs or pickup trucks—and got there first with new plug-in models while the company was waiting for obvious signs that American motorists were ready to make the switch.

"EV adoption can only hurt us one way, which is internal combustion sales go down and we don't have the electric vehicles to replace them and customers go somewhere else," Jacobson said.

Barra drove all of that, he said. She was willing to take the risk starting in 2017 and kept pushing the team to bet even more. As the gamble looked more secure in terms of consumer interest, she figured GM would be able to make vehicles that would win out over competitors. In other words, the conversion to electrification would have winners and losers, and she was determined to make sure GM was a winner.

Barra was so certain about the future for electric vehicles that she was often uninterested in proposals for new gasoline models. An idea for a small, gasoline-powered pickup that would compete with Ford's Maverick was shot down because no one wanted to take a proposal to Barra if it didn't have a battery.

As big as the investment was, it was only part of Barra's bigger plan. She wanted to grow the automaker in a huge way.

On her watch, the company grew revenue in 2016 on the back of truck and SUV sales in North America and growth in China. Selling Opel the next year cut revenue, but GM managed a bit of growth in 2018. Since then, the UAW strike, Covid pandemic, and chip shortage have all conspired to shrink sales. But in normal times, Barra's GM has made modest revenue gains and become much more profitable.

What she wants is major growth, the kind that gets investors in a lather. The long-term plan Jacobson was talking about would end up being the most aggressive move the company made since Alfred Sloan went on the acquisition spree that got GM into Europe and Australia and bought new brands and companies in the US. Barra reckoned that by getting an electric version of just about every vehicle GM sold—which covers most of the vehicle market—the company could steal customers from rivals that didn't have an EV to offer in that market segment. She has a brief window of time to offer EVs for everyone before the competition and steal back market share that GM had lost over so many years.

Taken together, it was part of a bold plan to double revenue to $280 billion by 2030. It counted on revenue growth in auto sales of as much as $100 billion a year. To get there, GM planned to hit $90 billion a year in EV sales alone by then, and somewhere between $105 billion and $145 billion in sales on conventional vehicles. It also included a plan to make Cadillac's entire lineup electric by 2025 and return to Europe by selling the brand's EVs there.

GM was laying the groundwork for its EV revolution. In July, the company invested in lithium producer Controlled Thermal Resources and its mining project in California. Lithium is an essential element used in making EV batteries and GM wanted a source close to home. The world's largest lithium producers are Australia, Chile, and China. Later in the year,

GM secured deals with producers for other metals needed in battery production and the specialized magnets needed for electric motors.

The company also had been on a hiring binge for the tech talent needed to support Barra's plans for electric vehicles, self-driving systems, and the software that would connect drivers to the web from their cars. GM had grown its geek squad to about 15,000 software engineers.

"We started to bring that talent in house to control info-tainment, transform to more software engineers as more attrition occurred, and then restructure product development to get the software together," Barra said. "We've been on a tear. We've hired 8,000. They all code. Some are coding for OnStar, some are deep in the vehicles."

Barra described an increasingly young and tech-minded workforce. She said 40 percent of the people at GM's tech center have been with the company for less than five years. The company entered 2020 with a plan to hire another 10,000 software and tech employees.

"There's so much energy," she beamed.

GM was planning to offer an electric vehicle in nearly every one of the segments where it did business by 2028. The company would still offer gasoline versions, so they could keep buyers who weren't ready to make the switch. In 2021, GM sold more than forty models in the US, mostly gasoline burners. By 2028, the lineup would grow to more than fifty different nameplates and more than half would be electric.

The plan also had the company gunning for $50 billion in sales from autonomous technology, the BrightDrop electric delivery van business, and software-enabled services, which included different apps and subscriptions that GM was planning to peddle to its car buyers through its data pipeline into the vehicles.

Reuss said GM isn't just substituting electric vehicles for a gasoline version. He plans to sell both, running plants that make internal combustion vehicles while his assembly lines that make EVs ramp up to meet customer demand.

"We're looking to increase our market share and really getting after the margins," Reuss told me. "The way you can do it is through really agile manufacturing. A lot of these are not direct replacements for vehicles in the lineup, but rather additive. We are going to do things like Factory Zero (that's the Hamtramck plant), where we don't have to shut anything off like truck lines, while we bring a new electric truck out."

As GM was preparing to reveal the plan to Wall Street, the semiconductor shortage was hitting a fever pitch. GM showed strong results in the second quarter of the year and lost minimal production. But a Covid outbreak in Malaysia cut chip production there, forcing GM to cut production in the third quarter. Vehicle sales in the US fell by more than 30 percent, revenue sank by 25 percent to $26.8 billion, and net income plummeted 40 percent to $2.4 billion. Fourth-quarter sales took a big hit, too, as chips remained short.

With the chip industry maxed out—and the gestation period for new fab plants being at least a year—it didn't look like there would be a quick or easy solution. That would be a threat to GM's cash flow just as the company was betting on uncertain electric-vehicle adoption.

What's a body to do? Jacobson said there was no question from Barra about charging ahead. GM went ahead and announced the growth plan anyway on October 6.

"When we bring it all together and look at the capital requirements and look at the growth opportunities that everyone has across the organization, we determined very quickly that the ramp-up in capital was very affordable and was the right thing to do," Jacobson told me in an interview. "One of the proudest moments of my first year was the fact that, in the face of the adversity, the semiconductor crisis, we actually leaned into the long-term vision even more."

GM invited Wall Street analysts in for a two-day event. They had a day of financial presentations and another seeing new models at GM's proving ground in rural Milford, Michigan. The presentation was a culmination of years of work to lay the foundation for a new kind of auto company. It started with the Bolt and development of the battery that would be Ultium, the acquisition of Cruise and work on its self-driving software, and the addition of thousands of code writers, battery experts, and scientists who were previously at the company in small numbers.

Barra came out in a black leather jacket with the Cadillac Lyriq EV behind her. She talked about a GM that was culturally more dynamic than what people expect. She made a case that the company isn't just an automaker, but an operator of technology and software platforms that will host a variety of businesses and revenue opportunities.

"You will see unprecedented urgency, decisiveness, agility, and breadth in our culture, our strategy, our execution, and our determination to own the opportunities before us," she said. "GM is delivering the tech that redefines how people and goods are moved."

Barra even paid homage to Alfred Sloan's credo that GM's five primary brands—Chevy, Pontiac, Oldsmobile, Buick, and Cadillac—offered "a car for every purse and purpose." She said GM would be a leader "in electrification with more than thirty EVs planned by 2025, including options for every price point and lifestyle."

GM would spend two days telling TheStreet that they weren't just an industrial company biding its time and paying dividends until new automakers like Tesla and Rivian took over. Under Barra, the company would lead and grow.

"When you look at all of the investments we've been making for five years plus, that's what positions us today to really be in execution mode," Barra said at the event. "We have great confidence in our ability to grow revenues."

It was evident at GM's investor day that Reuss was Barra's true partner in the transformation of the company. After Barra's intro, Reuss took the stage to lay out how GM would lead in electric vehicles and build new businesses with software services piped into the car by cellular and the company's OnStar satellite service.

Reuss gave a succinct road map for the total transformation that started in 2015 and was coming to fruition in 2021. First was the restructuring overseas, then cutting unprofitable vehicle programs, he said. Then the company put its focus on internal combustion vehicles with high margins, which funded the electric push. Then the idea was to use the brash Hummer and stylish Lyriq—which he said had gotten a rosier response in customer research than any GM vehicle in history—to make a splash. After that, GM would push out a trail of mass-market vehicles like pickup trucks and family SUVs. Cruise would provide another avenue for growth, he said.

GM's marketing campaign for its EV push is "Everybody In," because the company will offer an electric version of everything in its dealer showrooms.

There was even a bit of trash talking, corporate style. While GM was developing Ultium as a platform for multiple vehicles, Ford had shoehorned a battery into the frame of its existing F-150 pickup and modified the truck to get to market faster than GM, Tesla, and Rivian. Reuss took a not-so-subtle shot at his crosstown foe.

"When we started down the path to all-electric, we had a crucial decision to invest in a dedicated all-electric platform and architecture that will have scale, flexibility, and solid profitability," he said. "That's what we have in Ultium. We're able to do things that you just can't do if you're just stuffing a battery into an existing vehicle. No one will be able to touch us in the battery-electric truck space."

The old Ford-versus-GM battle was taking a different shape in the opening round of the EV race. It was looking like Aesop's tortoise against the hare. Ford got its truck and the Mustang Mach-E, which competes with Tesla's Model Y, to market before GM. Both are on platforms that will only host those vehicles. GM spent the time putting building blocks in place with Ultium. It has a platform that can be adjusted, like a set of Legos, to make vehicles big and small. Everything from a small Chevy Equinox SUV to a huge Hummer. Ultium, which is a separate company half owned by GM, also started building battery plants ahead of Ford. Once the blocks are in place, GM will begin a building blitz of new electric models. That blitz was enabled by the methodical process of putting the pieces in place to commercialize the Ultium pack. Meanwhile, Ford got there first with the F-150 Lightning.

The way Reuss explained Ultium, it's not just a battery. It's a tapestry that GM and its designers can use to create every size and type of vehicle. He said it also frees the company's stylists from some of the constraints of internal combustion vehicles.

Designers have to make room to house a big engine up front and a transmission and drive shaft tunneled through the middle of the vehicle. Freed of those constraints, they may be able to do more with vehicle shapes and interior space.

Reuss and Barra both talked about the software in the car. Rather than let Google and Apple connect with consumers via their smartphones, GM was hatching a plan to create its own software-enabled services that would be connected to the Internet via the cellular pipeline into GM's cars.

Alan Wexler, the company's senior vice president of innovation, whom Barra hired from digital consulting firm Publicis Sapient, made his pitch for GM's software capabilities. GM did extensive customer research, Wexler said, and found that they would pay about $135 a month on products and services after they bought their car. By 2030, GM would have 30 million connected vehicles on the road.

That meant the company saw a market for such products and services at $80 billion, of which GM "sees possible revenue of $20 to $25 billion," Wexler said. The margins could be great, too. OnStar's $2 billion a year in revenue is a fraction of GM's $140 billion. But with 70 percent profit margins, it's close to 20 percent of net income.

OnStar would power GM's budding insurance business by offering better rates for drivers who behave on the roads. That could bring in $6 billion in annual revenue, Wexler said. GM was already selling its Super Cruise system, which lets Cadillac owners drive and change lanes on the highway with their hands off the wheel. An advanced version called Ultra Cruise goes on sale in 2023. Both would be enabled by GM's growing software capabilities and the satellite connection to GM's vehicles.

Ammann came on later to talk about Cruise. At this point, autonomous vehicles as a business had never failed to disappoint. Companies had talked about plans to get self-driving vehicles on the road to act as taxis or robot-driven rivals to Uber or delivering packages and food in late 2019 or 2020. They all missed their targets.

Even Waymo, which was ferrying people around a tiny enclave of the Phoenix suburb of Chandler, had just a modest deployment of its cars. And Chandler is a facile driving assignment with light traffic and broad residential roads.

Some had gone out of business due to lack of funding. Others sold out to big companies with deep pockets. Startup Zoox Inc. had its software running in Toyota Highlander SUVs in San Francisco. But after a tough funding round, the company sold to Amazon. Another startup called Voyage had successfully started a business moving senior citizens around the massive elderly community The Village in Florida but sold to Cruise when cash funding needs became more daunting.

After several years of autonomous technology bumbling and stumbling along, Ammann said Cruise was just about ready to go. As soon as the GM unit got permission from the California Public Utility Commission, it would be charging for rides in self-driven Chevy Bolt EVs around the city. That would happen in 2022. From there, Ammann said, Cruise would deploy the Origin, a dedicated four- to six-passenger shuttle designed for self-driving services. That would enable the company to expand across the US by 2025.

He said Cruise would be able to follow Uber's path to $50 billion in revenue in six years. Uber actually had $50 billion in gross billings, with its drivers taking home most of the money. With no drivers, Cruise would keep that money and posted margins of around 40 percent.

"This thing we have all felt is still science fiction is about to become science fact," he said. "In three to four years, we'll be deployed in multiple cities and in multiple markets. When you look out five to six years from now, we'll be in every place you can imagine around the US and multiple places around the world."

GM's growth plan was so big and so broad that it stretched credibility. The whole presentation was about as un-Mary as it can get. First, doubling revenue from an old industrial company is a massive goal. Barra was months away from turning sixty and would be retired before it was determined whether

GM would meet its goal. Targets like this are often missed, and they are made so far in advance that no one even remembers that they were made. The CEO is rarely held accountable.

That said, under Barra, GM had rock-solid credibility with investors. The company almost always hit or beat its earnings guidance and usually bested earnings estimates unless there was an unforeseen problem, like a semiconductor shortage. GM hits targets because they are realistic. This was different.

"It was done in a way that's very Mary," Barra said later. "We have a plan to back it up. I don't put out wishes and hopes and dreams. You've got to have substance behind it. The plans that we shared, there are plans behind it. It's very Mary."

Despite her credibility, there were definitely doubters. The stock fell almost 1 percent that day, which is surprising given that it had the three ingredients investors loved: lots of EVs, a date certain on autonomous vehicle services, and growth in software-based subscription services with high profit margins. Growth!

So what gives? While Barra was admired, the goals were so big that investors didn't know what to make of it. The numbers were too big to be taken seriously.

Jonas wrote after the presentation that GM would be valued at as much as $200 billion if the company was a startup because "few companies, in our opinion, are in a position to display the same breadth of capability across EV, AV, manufacturing, services, and connected car as GM is today. All the pieces are under the GM corporate umbrella."

Given the muted reaction, Jonas said that industry watchers give "extremely low probability these targets are achieved."

In other words, despite all she had achieved, Barra would just have to prove that GM could pull this off.

EPILOGUE

As 2022 got underway, the second phase of Barra's transformation was in full view. She had revealed her plan to double revenue. The battery plant in Lordstown was nearly ready to start production. Her old factory in Hamtramck was building the electric Hummer, and another plant in Ontario was preparing to make electric delivery vans that could go 250 miles on a charge while carrying packages for the likes of UPS and FedEx. The former Saturn facility in Tennessee was also starting to make the Cadillac Lyriq.

GM was fully prepared for the electric future and Cruise was strongly positioned for whatever would come next with self-driving cars. The company had scrapped most of its underperforming businesses. As capital markets started tightening, Barra had the money to fund her ambition to make GM a technology leader. The company was ready to meet whatever changes were coming.

But was GM getting too ready? Electric vehicle sales were growing, but only among luxury buyers. GM would be first to test whether Middle America was ready to go electric, give up gasoline, and jump on the nation's inadequate charging network. The dearth of charging stations wouldn't be a barrier forever, but it is creating resistance among many drivers. By diverting so much of its budget to EVs, Barra's plan risks leaving behind the people who don't have the means or desire to make the switch.

Reuss, who is emerging as Barra's heir apparent, countered that GM has advantages that can safeguard its shift to high-tech cars. The company's network of factories was prepared to build EVs and autonomous vehicles, but some of them could also make conventional models if EV sales didn't materialize. The Tennessee plant is making the electric Lyriq and gasoline SUVs. While Hamtramck builds an electric Hummer and GM prepares to make an electric Silverado, Reuss still has all of his truck plants making gasoline-burning pickups. A transition can be staggered plant by plant.

If GM can pull it off, it will be a long road to redemption for the company that killed off the EV1. The engineers working for Barra and Reuss have more experience developing electric cars than many competitors. Some of them were around to build the EV1, and many others developed the Volt and Bolt. Ford didn't have that experience. Neither did Toyota nor Volkswagen.

GM also had an edge on startups like Rivian and Lucid Motors. They needed to bootstrap a company, build new plants, assemble a workforce, and learn automaking from scratch. They need to raise cash from Wall Street. GM's truck and SUV business prints money. Those plants are funding GM's EV push. Barra doesn't have to sell more stock or borrow money to pay for it.

When it came to self-driving vehicles, Waymo was the closest rival to GM's Cruise in the race to create robotically-chauffeured rides. GM is first to get approval to charge fares in San Francisco to ferry people around in a car with no driver.

There was a waiting list to take autonomous rides. Waymo was close to doing the same, but the Google unit didn't own its vehicles or have plants to build them. The company would have to rely on deals with carmakers to build out the business. Only Argo, the startup co-owned by VW and Ford, could build its own cars and was even close to GM and Waymo with autonomous technology. Most startups had died off or sold out. Now the hard part: Growing it to $50 billion.

With connected vehicles, only Tesla was better than GM. Musk had been giving his customers upgrades to their cars and delivering infotainment over the air for years. Even though OnStar was often overlooked as an asset at GM, the unit's $2 billion a year in revenue was hugely profitable and its satellites were capable of much more. OnStar was seen mostly as a safety service for drivers, alerting 911 responders when airbags were deployed and the like. GM was preparing to deliver so much more via that data pipeline.

Barra says no other company has the broad portfolio of assets to succeed in the next era of transportation. She has a strong argument.

But, hey, it's GM. There is often drama. As successful as Barra has been and as respected as she is, the world just isn't ready to buy the GM story. Not yet. The fact that the stock dropped the day Barra unveiled her plan to double revenue says that investors don't think she can pull it off and will wait for signs that the company can do it. The Morgan Stanley analyst Adam Jonas said GM carried "execution risk." That's Wall Street speak that says this company may not be able to finish the transformation. That was a rough judgment from Jonas, who had spent several years lavishing Barra and GM with praise.

Investors had bought the GM story to a certain degree. GM's stock rose 45 percent from Barra's start as CEO in

January 2014 to early 2022 before the market tumbled. While commendable, that brings up a big question: If GM has the right strategy and all the pieces in place, why isn't it valued like Tesla? For that matter, the company still wasn't valued as much as Toyota? Why can't GM get more respect?

In part, it's because the company still has a business making internal-combustion vehicles that is on the way out. It's only a question of how long before it evaporates. GM and its historic rivals make their money in a business that increasingly seems so yesteryear. Since the growth is in EVs, all of those plants and machines that make carbon-emitting vehicles are waiting to become obsolete and essentially worthless. Or so says the investment thesis against GM and in favor of the new auto companies like Tesla, Rivian, and Lucid.

The other is that, this is GM. The company has a record of missteps and is historically very cautious. Even when GM is out in front with an idea, it sometimes moves too slowly and without confidence. GM started OnStar to connect its cars to a satellite data pipeline in 1996, but never got the most out of it. The EV1 predated the founding of Tesla by seven years, but GM didn't move past it and let Musk upend transportation. Akerson approved the Bolt in 2012 and Barra made sure its battery was competitive when it went on sale in 2016. It was a great start, but GM didn't come up with an encore for another six years even as Tesla was creating an advantage in electric vehicle technology and building profits, creating a powerhouse brand, and branching out its charging network.

Barra's plan will break that habit if she can instill a culture that sticks to its ambition and keeps pushing beyond her tenure. That's one reason the company hasn't fully gotten credit for the foundation that she and Reuss have been putting in place. Investors and some consumers—especially the affluent coastal types who eschew the likes of Chevy and Ford—need to be convinced to fully trust General Motors. The message seems to be, "Yeah, good plan. It could work. Show me."

Throughout 2021, GM was hit by a series of setbacks that gave the doubters more questions than answers. The Bolt's battery, which was completely designed and assembled by LG Chem, had a rare defect that caused it to catch on fire. The problem began getting more serious in late 2020 when GM recalled about 69,000 of the cars. But the problem wouldn't go away.

In July of 2021, the company had to recall the same 69,000 cars for the second time in a year because the first fix didn't work. GM and LG discovered a manufacturing defect in the cells that caused a short. When that short happens, it sets off a spark, generates heat, and the cells catch fire. GM wasn't the only company with battery fires. Tesla, Korea's Hyundai, and Volkswagen also had them.

GM just had a few more of them. Those fires were unnerving for car owners because the vehicles went up in flames while charging in the garage, not as a result of an accident or any kind of impact. No one was injured, but there was a spontaneous blaze in nineteen Bolts. When electric vehicles catch fire, they burn at more than 1,700 degrees. They are difficult to put out and the cars end up burnt to a cinder.

Barra did the right thing and recalled all 142,000 Bolts that had ever been built, taking a cue from her ignition switch playbook. But for most of the year, a solution was elusive; GM and LG didn't have batteries to replace what was in the vehicles on the road.

As a result, GM had to resort to some embarrassing, but prudent measures to protect its customers while engineers at the automaker and partner LG raced to find a real fix. One measure was a software upgrade that limited the total charge to 90 percent and not run it all the way down, which meant

Bolt owners could only drive a fraction of the 238 miles that the car promised. They were also told not to store the car inside overnight. At one point, GM told owners to park fifty feet away from other cars if they were in a public space.

In October, nearly a year after the first recall, GM and LG found a solution and started producing new battery packs to replace the old ones. It cost $1.9 billion, with LG absorbing most of the cost. GM squarely blamed LG and said that even though the two partnered for the future Ultium batteries, GM would be designing the pack and the manufacturing process.

That means that when the Hummer pickup and Cadillac Lyriq go on sale using the Ultium pack, GM can't fail. The company would have no one to blame. And in fairness, when GM made the Chevy Volt plug-in hybrid, it had no battery issues. GM had a much bigger hand in developing those cells and assembling the packs.

There was another threat to GM getting out ahead of the competition and stealing buyers. Aside from the fact that Tesla built a lead and sold close to 1 million EVs in 2021 (and was building two new plants), Ford had stolen a march on GM with the Mach-E and Lightning. Korea's Hyundai and Kia also had some exciting EVs for sale. For most of the year, GM only had the Bolt, which was grounded due to the recall.

The Mach-E's top battery boasted 305 miles of range on a charge, which is competitive with Tesla's Model Y, and beats the Bolt. And it was far more stylish than the Chevy offering. GM will mount a big push with the electric Silverado pickup, and battery-powered versions of the sporty Chevy Blazer and Equinox family SUV in 2023.

It's early in the electric race, of course. But GM was seen as the most aggressive contender to Tesla and had been telling its electrification story, nay, hyping it since 2017. Ford, which is on its third CEO in four years, got out ahead. By 2025, GM's tortoise-like plan to get Ultium in place has forecasters predicting its EV sales will be second only to Tesla's, but it shows just how difficult it will be to pull off Barra's plan to steal market share and become a leader in this race.

Even as GM was starting to build the Hummer and Lyriq, the company had lost control of the story that it was on the cutting edge of electrification. While the Hummer was finding buyers, environmentalists lambasted it because the 9,100-pound behemoth used so much power. Safety hawks fretted that it would maul other cars on the road.

"The narrative would be very different externally if we did not have the Bolt recall," Barra said. "We aren't just starting to get EVs out, we're just starting to get EVs off the Ultium platform out. We had a pause when we had defects from LG Chem. We do have vehicles out there. We have for years. The reason I feel confident that we're in a leadership position and we will lead is we've made the investments in the Ultium platform. It's giving us the ability to do a portfolio of vehicles."

Barra took some heat among the Twitterati over GM's EV plan. When President Joe Biden was in Detroit, praising GM as a leader in electric drive, he didn't mention a word about Tesla. That's mostly politics. Elon Musk is an anti-union billionaire, not exactly a hero to Democrats. While Barra did nothing to feed Biden's errant view that GM—not Tesla—was the leader, she became the butt of a slew of memes and jokes found under #MaryLed. One had her face imposed on that of a salesman peddling an electric car from 1913.

Another event shook some of the faith in GM's ability to erase its past. On December 16, as Ammann was preparing for morning meetings at Cruise, he got a call from Barra. After months of tension over how to execute the Cruise mission of providing autonomous vehicles and ride services, and whether to take the company public, she told him he was out. Fired.

Cruise's strategy is a big part of Barra's growth plan. Ammann had talked about building self-driving vehicles that individual consumers could buy. GM and Cruise also discussed the possibility of making BrightDrop's electric delivery vans capable of self-drive. And Cruise's talented staff could work to enhance Super Cruise and Ultra Cruise, the hands-free driving service sold in GM models.

Ammann pitched the vision, so he clearly agreed. But internally, he wanted to focus on the robotaxi business before spreading too far, too fast into other projects. He had also pressed Barra on an IPO for Cruise. It would give the company more financial firepower to build the business, but perhaps more important, it would give Cruise a stock to offer its top talent and new hires. Crucially, it would also give him more autonomy running the company.

Barra wasn't having it. Cruise is fully funded and she and Jacobson both say the company is better fully integrated with GM for the time being. Plus, with no revenue and a choppy stock market, 2022 ended up being no time to sell new shares. Over the course of Cruise's board meeting on November 2 and that fateful call on December 16, Barra and Ammann had some tough conversations, say people close to the situation. Their relationship had been souring for some time, they said. GM's board had enlisted Goldman Sachs to review options, and its bankers said they should keep Cruise. Ammann made Cruise employees available for Goldman's review. Other banks had pitched GM and Ammann on an IPO, which he was keen to do. With GM management siding with Goldman and Ammann wanting to move ahead with an IPO, friction grew between him and Barra. GM also wanted better working collaboration between the two companies. Barra had enough and he was ousted.

Investors hated the news. GM shares traded down 5.5 percent on the first trading after it was announced. Ammann wasn't just any executive. He was the outside voice that helped GM look at its business with fresh eyes and a sharp scalpel. His overture to Peugeot CEO Carlos Tavares resulted in the Opel sale. He also spearheaded the acquisition of Cruise.

GM's initial press release was served cold. "General Motors Co. announced today that Dan Ammann, Chief Executive Officer of Cruise, is leaving the company. Kyle Vogt, Cruise President and Chief Technical Officer, will serve as interim CEO."

Not another word about Ammann's contributions to Barra's transformation plan at GM. He had been a big part of it. Barra and Reuss come from a lifetime at GM and a similar background. Thinking as a different kind of car company will test them both. When asked about losing Ammann's outside view, Barra responded that GM had hired more outsiders. Jacobson, her CFO, came from Delta Airlines. So did Gil West, chief operating officer of Cruise.

Taken separately, none of the setbacks in the second half of 2021 derail GM's push to grow the business and become what Barra wants: a great new-era car company. But it does show how fragile momentum is and how difficult this transition will be.

The Bolt battery fires and impasse with Ammann make it seem like GM suffers from some kind of generational curse. I asked Barra if she felt that way at times of crisis. She laughed. "No, I don't," she said. "I think there's no business that's easy to run these days. Whether it's supply chain or Covid, or transformation or technology or new startups or other industries coming into your business. With the Bolt, our engineers persevered to find the cause. When I was promoted to CEO and I had to deal with ignition switch recall, that was totally different. That was someone who did not have the curiosity a decade prior to say, 'Wait a minute, there's something happening here that I don't exactly understand.' A great engineer is curious."

Barra is curious and she is imaginative enough to have created this vision for a new GM, one that grows and wins instead of downsizing for survival. After years of decline, near death, and struggle for redemption, GM will finally post some real growth. Doubling revenue is unlikely, not with 100 new electric vehicles from all carmakers coming to market by the end of 2024. Barra has put together a credible and aggressive plan, and one that should work.

In September, GM put a debut edition of the Lyriq up online and opened reservations. It sold 2,000 in nineteen minutes. A similar number of the Hummer EV sold out in ten minutes. GM can rebuild a relationship with wealthy buyers. Cadillac had 200,000 people express interest in the Lyriq online.

The Lyriq and GM's plan for an electric Escalade have a real shot to lead Cadillac back into the hearts of wealthy Americans. The brand has already shown strong growth in China. It's vital for Barra's push. Early in the year, GM was seeing so much demand for the Lyriq and Hummer that the company decided to boost production. By June, the Lyriq had sold out all of the 2023 model year. Cadillac has a potential hit with its first EV. The plan is gaining traction.

GM saw growth in commercial trucks and vans, too. It got out early with the BrightDrop van, which is cheaper than Ford's E-Transit and goes more miles on a charge. FedEx was the first to line up, taking delivery of 500 vans in December.

At the Consumer Electronics Show in January 2021, Barra took the stage to show off the new electric Silverado. It will come to market a year after Ford's truck, but it will be more capable. Ford's Lightning can go 300 miles on a charge and tow 10,000 pounds. The Silverado, Barra said, will go 400 miles and a work version of the truck will be able to tow 8,000 pounds. Later on, Chevy will have a version that can tow 20,000, which beats gasoline-powered pickups. Chevy even bragged that the pickup bed is almost six inches longer than Ford's. Truck wars get ugly!

The electric truck battle underscores a key difference between Barra and crosstown competitor Jim Farley, the CEO of Ford. Farley, a gifted marketer, has retrofitted the F-150 truck with batteries to move first and put an electric halo over Ford's brand. Barra and Reuss took their time and developed Ultium to transform every vehicle they make. Farley generated buzz. Barra is methodical.

GM's boldest move will be selling lower-priced electric Chevys. As of this writing, the average EV costs $65,000 and many of them are the third vehicle in some affluent family's garage. But Barra wants "Everybody In," as GM's tagline goes. The Equinox and Blazer will sell as cheaply as $30,000. She may have blown up Sloan's global empire, but she is all in on selling electric cars "for every purse and purpose."

GM will be prepared for the changes that are coming, Reuss told me, because the company spent time developing an Ultium battery that is so versatile and because GM is getting its battery plants up quickly. The Ultium battery will enable GM to make EVs at a similar cost to gasoline-burning models, Reuss said. One big endorsement: Honda partnered with GM to use the technology for its EVs.

"To get to a $30,000 Equinox-like vehicle—that's our second highest volume vehicle—you really need to get the battery cell plants up and running and you need to do it in a way that you can start slow and ramp fast," Reuss said.

By the end of 2023, GM will have two battery plants open. Ford's don't come online until 2025. GM will likely have better access to EV batteries well before most competitors. That's a big reason why Reuss and Barra feel that their strategy to make purpose-built EVs will win.

That may be one of the most important and risky aspects of Barra's plan. It comes with a public commitment to make GM's vehicles all electric by 2035. The company is laying the groundwork before there are clear signs that all buyers want to plug in. The plan to sell lower-price electric vehicles to middle America in 2023 will be a major milestone to converting to electric drive. If Barra pulls that off, she will be one of the key figures in the change to clean transportation and will have transformed the company. I asked Reuss if part of his passion for the company was to return it to greatness, like the early days of his career. He corrected me.

"You mentioned when the company was great," he said. "I'm not sure I was there. I joined in 1986, which was a pretty tough time. Every year it was a restructuring and a reduction. For me it does mean a lot. We saw a lot of the consolidation. Then of course our bankruptcy and our emergence. It means a ton for me and anyone who has been at the company during that period of time."

Barra has a similar motivation to see out the mission, to bring GM back.

"I had no idea coming out of bankruptcy that I would have this opportunity, but I knew that I wanted to be part of the team that was going to build GM into the company that I knew it could be," she said. "That's what motivates me every day."

NOTES

CHAPTER 1

1. Maggie McGrath, "Mary Barra Named GM CEO, Automaker's First Female Chief," *Forbes*, December 10, 2013, https://www .forbes.com/sites/maggiemcgrath/2013/12/10/mary-barra -named-as-new-gm-ceo-becoming-first-female-chief-for-the -automaker/?sh=15f3237b642e.
2. Jeff Bennett and Sara Murray, "General Motors Names Mary Barra as CEO," *Wall Street Journal*, December 10, 2013, https://www.wsj.com/articles/SB10001424052702303560204579249952766187032.
3. Dominic Rushe, "Mary Barra Named GM CEO to Become America's First Female Car Chief," *The Guardian*, December 10, 2013, https://www.theguardian.com/business/2013/dec/10/gm -mary-barra-ceo-first-woman-car.
4. "GM's 'Dog Ate My Homework' Must End, Barra Says, As Recall Fades," Bloomberg, September 29, 2015, https://www .bloomberg.com/news/articles/2015-09-28/gm-s-dog-ate-my -homework-must-end-barra-says-as-recall-fades.

CHAPTER 2

1. Laura Colby, *Road to Power: How GM's Mary Barra Shattered the Glass Ceiling* (Wiley, 2015), p. 8.
2. Laura Colby, *Road to Power*, p. 64.
3. Laura Colby, *Road to Power*, p. 64.
4. John Pearley Huffman, "Remember the Fiero," *Car and Driver*, October 19, 2019, https://www.caranddriver.com/features /columns/a29513894/remember-the-fiero/.
5. "Pontiac Drops the Fire-Plagued Fiero," *Automotive News*, March 1, 2016, https://www.autonews.com/article/20160301 /CCHISTORY/160229863/pontiac-drops-the-fire-plagued -fiero?adobe_mc=MCMID%3D6773929136394764475709851 2261825727088%7CMCORGID%3D138FFF2554E6E7220A4C 98C6%2540AdobeOrg%7CTS%3D1625239987&CSAuthResp =1%3A%3A682552%3A20989%3A24%3Asuccess%3AFEE75 BC908B6501B50047305FADE71DC.
6. Stephen Miller, "GM Chief Tried to Transform Auto Maker but Couldn't Halt Its Decline," *Wall Street Journal*, December 1, 2007, https://www.wsj.com/articles/SB119643745545909591.
7. Robert J. Cole, "G.M. to Acquire Hughes Aircraft in $5 Billion Bid," *New York Times*, June 6, 1985, https://www.nytimes .com/1985/06/06/us/gm-to-acquire-hughes-aircraft-in-5 -billion-bid.html.
8. Paul A. Eisenstein, "GM's Saturn Division Reports First Profit, Ignoring Capital Cost," *Christian Science Monitor*, August 2, 1993, https://www.csmonitor.com/1993/0802/02082.html.
9. David Kushma and Nunzio Lupo, "GM Net Off 69%," *Washington Post*, February 6, 1987, https://www.washingtonpost .com/archive/business/1987/02/06/gm-net-off-69/8034bccd -f3aa-420a-9911-f7f59d5da9a0/.
10. Warren Brown and Frank Swoboda, "Stempel Steps Down as Chairman of GM," *Washington Post*, October 27, 1992, https://www.washingtonpost.com/archive/politics/1992/10 /27/stempel-steps-down-as-chairman-of-gm/1f05f153 -19b8-46ee-b588-198aeca6e746/.

11. Laura Colby, *Road to Power*, p. 64.

12. Amy Crawford, "Can Poletown Come Back After a General Motors Shutdown?" Bloomberg CityLab, December 10, 2018, https://www.bloomberg.com/news/articles/2018-12-10 /the-history-of-gm-poletown-and-its-impact-on-detroit.

CHAPTER 3

1. David Welch, "GM—A View from the Back Seat," Bloomberg, June 2, 2009, https://www.bloomberg.com/news/articles/2009 -06-02/gm-a-view-from-the-back-seat.

2. "Saturn: Still Tiny, but Bleeding Like a Monster," Bloomberg, June 1, 2003, https://www.bloomberg.com/news/articles/2003-06-01 /saturn-still-tiny-but-bleeding-like-a-monster.

3. "Harbour Report 2005: GM Leads Seven of 13 Segments; Three Out of Top Five Assembly Plants Overall," Automotive Intelligence, June 2, 2005, https://www.autointell.com/nao _companies/general_motors/gm-manufacturing/harbour -reports/gm-harbour-2005.htm.

4. "Commentary: Detroit Is Over a ($50) Barrel," Bloomberg, September 12, 2004, https://www.bloomberg.com/news /articles/2004-09-12/commentary-detroit-is-over-a-50-barrel.

5. "GM Slashing 30,000 Jobs, Closing Plants," NBC News, November 21, 2005, https://www.nbcnews.com/id/wbna10138507.

6. David Welch, "The Battle Raging Inside GM," Bloomberg, December 2, 2009, https://www.bloomberg.com/news/articles /2009-12-02/the-battle-raging-inside-gm.

CHAPTER 4

1. David C. Smith, "GM's 'Hands-On' Engine Whiz: Tom Stephens Grew Up with Grease Under His Fingernails," Ward'sAuto, March 1, 1996, https://www.wardsauto.com/news-analysis /gms-hands-engine-whiz-tom-stephens-grew-grease-under -his-fingernails.

CHAPTER 5

1. Rana Faroohar, "Mary Barra's Bumpy Ride at the Wheel of GM," *TIME*, September 25, 2014, https://time.com/magazine/us/3429641/october-6th-2014-vol-184-no-13-u-s/.

2. "News Conference on General Motors Ignition Switch Recall," C-SPAN video, April 1, 2014, https://www.c-span.org/video/?318642-1/victims-families-news-conference-gm-recall&event=318642&playEvent.

3. Rana Faroohar, "Mary Barra's Bumpy Ride at the Wheel of GM."

4. "GM Said to Oust VP, Lawyer After Valukas Review," Bloomberg, June 5, 2014, https://www.bloomberg.com/news/articles/2014-06-05/gm-said-to-oust-senior-lawyer-bill-kemp-following-valukas-review.

5. "GM Executives Help Scour Social Media Seeking Vehicle Flaws," Bloomberg Law, November 26, 2014, https://news.bloomberglaw.com/product-liability-and-toxics-law/gm-executives-help-scour-social-media-seeking-vehicle-flaws.

CHAPTER 6

1. David Welch and Bryan Gruley, "GM's Mary Barra Bets Big on an Electric, Self-Driving Future," *Bloomberg Businessweek*, September 19, 2019, https://www.bloomberg.com/news/features/2019-09-19/before-gm-goes-electric-mary-barra-has-a-strike-to-settle.

2. Norihiko Shirouzu, "GM to Shut Plant, Cut Jobs in Indonesia, Where Japanese Dominate," Reuters, February 26, 2015, https://www.reuters.com/article/us-autos-gm-indonesia/gm-to-shut-plant-cut-jobs-in-indonesia-where-japanese-dominate-idUSKBN0LU0S720150226.

CHAPTER 7

1. David Welch and Bryan Gruley, "GM's Mary Barra Bets Big on an Electric, Self-Driving Future."

CHAPTER 8

1. Allison Martell and Allison Lampert, "Canada Blindsided by GM Closure, Workers Walk Out in Protest," Reuters, November 26, 2018, https://www.reuters.com/article/us-gm-restructuring-canada/canada-blindsided-by-gm-closure-workers-walk-out-in-protest-idUSKCN1NV21H.
2. Jamie L. LaReau, "Canadian Union Slams GM in Ads Over Oshawa Plant Closing," *Detroit Free Press*, December 20, 2018, https://www.freep.com/story/money/cars/general-motors/2018/12/20/general-motors-unifor-canada-plant-closures/2362845002/.
3. "GM's Electric Future Means Prosperity for One Michigan Town, Disaster for Another," Bloomberg, October 8, 2019, https://www.bloomberg.com/news/features/2019-10-08/gm-s-electric-future-means-prosperity-or-ruin-for-michigan-towns.
4. Mike Colias, "GM's Plan to Cut Jobs and Plants Draws Fire from Trump, Others," *Wall Street Journal*, December 26, 2018, https://www.wsj.com/articles/gm-says-it-will-cut-15-of-salaried-workforce-in-north-america-1543246232.
5. "GM Pays Barra $21.9 Million as Trump, Biden Attack Closings," Bloomberg, April 18, 2019, https://www.bloomberg.com/news/articles/2019-04-18/gm-pays-ceo-barra-21-9-million-as-trump-biden-attack-closings.

CHAPTER 9

1. "Trump Threatens to Cut GM's Electric Car Subsidies Because of Plant Closures," Associated Press, November 27, 2018, https://www.cbc.ca/news/business/trump-gm-electric-cars-1.4922802.
2. Randy Ludlow, "Trump, in Youngstown, Says Jobs Are Coming Back to Ohio," *Columbus Dispatch*, July 26, 2017, https://www.dispatch.com/story/news/politics/election/national/2017/07/26/trump-in-youngstown-says-jobs/20069140007/.
3. Ben Popken, "Trump Threatens GM's Subsidies After Layoff Announcement," NBC News, November 27, 2018, https://

www.nbcnews.com/business/autos/trump-threatens-slap-gm
-subsidies-after-layoff-announcement-n940726.

4. "Uber Tries to Stand Up to Trump While Working with Him,"
Bloomberg, January 31, 2017, https://www.bloomberg.com
/opinion/articles/2017-01-30/uber-tries-to-stand-up-to-trump
-while-working-with-him.

5. Danielle Mouio, "Elon Musk Accidentally Tweeted Trump's
'Immigration Ban Is Not Right'—Then Deleted It," *Business
Insider*, February 15, 2017, https://www.businessinsider.com
/elon-musk-deletes-tweet-saying-trump-immigration-ban-is
-not-right-2017-2.

6. "Bill Ford's Struggle to Stay Friends with Donald Trump,"
Bloomberg, February 3, 2017, https://www.bloomberg.com
/news/articles/2017-02-03/bromance-between-bill-ford-and
-trump-hits-snag-over-immigration.

7. David Gelles, Kate Kelly, Rachel Abrams, and Michael Cork-
ery, "Rift Widens Between Trump and Business Leaders,"
New York Times, August 15, 2017, https://www.nytimes.com
/2017/08/15/business/trump-councils-ceos.html.

8. David Gelles, Kate Kelly, Rachel Abrams, and Michael Cork-
ery, "Rift Widens Between Trump and Business Leaders."

9. David A. Graham, "Why Isn't Trump Helping the Autoworkers?"
The Atlantic, September 17, 2019, https://www.theatlantic.com
/ideas/archive/2019/09/where-trump-gm-strike/598189/.

10. "Inside GM's Four-Week Sprint to Build Emergency Ventilators,"
Bloomberg, March 30, 2020, https://www.bloomberg.com
/news/articles/2020-03-30/inside-gm-s-four-week-sprint-to
-build-emergency-ventilators.

11. "GM Forges on Without US Ventilator Contract After Trump
Attack," Bloomberg, March 27, 2020, https://www.bloomberg
.com/news/articles/2020-03-27/trump-threatens-to-force
-gm-to-move-faster-on-ventilators.

12. "Trump Says GM 'Doing a Fantastic Job' After White House
Threat," Bloomberg, March 29, 2020, https://www.bloomberg
.com/news/articles/2020-03-29/trump-says-gm-doing-a
-fantastic-job-after-white-house-threat.

CHAPTER 18

1. Edward Lapham, "John DeLorean Remembered: He Was Larger Than Life, and He Knew It, Too," *Automotive News*, March 20, 2005, https://www.autoweek.com/news/a2076581/john -delorean-remembered-he-was-larger-life-and-he-knew-it-too/.

2. "The 1972 Lordstown Strike," Walter P. Reuther Library, Wayne State University, August 12, 2013, http://reuther.wayne .edu/node/10756.

3. Agis Salpukas, "U.S. Steel to Close Youngstown Mills; Timing Is Uncertain," *New York Times*, January 4, 1978, https:// www.nytimes.com/1978/01/04/archives/us-steel-to-close -youngstown-mills-timing-is-uncertain-competitive.html.

4. https://www.ohiosteel.org/ohio-steel-industry/history /#1970s.

5. Michael Roknick, "GM to Suspend 3rd Shift at Lordstown Plant," *The Herald*, November 10, 2016, https://www.sharonherald .com/news/gm-to-suspend-3rd-shift-at-lordstown-plant /article_d76af277-3fb9-536d-a078-df0e36f01e0e.html.

6. "GM Squeezed $118 Million from Its Ohio Workers, Then Shut the Plant," Bloomberg, March 29, 2019, https://www.bloomberg .com/news/articles/2019-03-29/gm-brushed-off-union -concessions-before-idling-ohio-car-plant.

7. "Lordstown Motors CEO Steve Burns Responds to Allegations from Short-Seller Hindenburg," CNBC video, March 18, 2021, https://www.cnbc.com/video/2021/03/18/lordstown-motors -ceo-steve-burns-responds-to-allegations-from-short-seller -hindenburg.html.

8. "Lordstown to Sell Ohio Plant to Foxconn in $280 Million Deal," Bloomberg, September 30, 2021, https://www.bloomberg.com /news/articles/2021-09-30/lordstown-to-sell-ohio-plant -to-foxconn-in-280-million-deal#:~:text=Lordstown%20 Motors%20Corp.,also%20receiving%20an%20equity%20 investment.

CHAPTER 11

1. "Self-Driving Cars, in 1956?" GM Heritage Center, 2019, https://www.gmheritagecenter.com/featured/Autonomous _Vehicles.html.

2. Hope King, "Google's New Self-Driving Cars Hit the Road," CNN Business, May 15, 2015, https://money.cnn.com/2015/05 /15/technology/google-car-prototype/?iid=EL.

3. "How GM Bought Its Way to the Front of the Driverless-Car Pack," Bloomberg, November 30, 2017, https://www.bloomberg .com/news/articles/2017-11-30/how-gm-bought-its-way-to -the-front-of-the-driverless-car-pack.

4. "A Slow Ride in the First Self-Driving Chevy Bolt," Bloomberg, November 29, 2017, https://www.bloomberg.com/news /articles/2017-11-29/a-slow-ride-in-the-first-self-driving-chevy -bolt.

5. "Waymo Is 99% of the Way to Self-Driving Cars. The Last 1% Is the Hardest," Bloomberg, August 17, 2017, https://www .bloomberg.com/news/articles/2021-08-17/waymo-s-self -driving-cars-are-99-of-the-way-there-the-last-1-is-the-hardest.

CHAPTER 12

1. Danny Hakim, "A Campaign by the Sierra Club Chides General Motors About the Hummer's Gas Mileage," *New York Times*, July 29, 2003, https://www.nytimes.com/2003/07/29 /business/media-business-advertising-campaign-sierra-club -chides-general-motors-about.html.

2. "Amazon-Backed Rivian Spurned GM with Plans to Build for Others," Bloomberg, April 17, 2019, https://www.bloomberg .com/news/articles/2019-04-17/amazon-backed-rivian -spurned-gm-with-plans-to-build-for-others.

3. Mike Colias and Ben Foldy, "How Ford Won the Race for Rivian," *Wall Street Journal*, November 16, 2021, https://www.wsj .com/articles/how-ford-won-the-race-for-rivian-11636171218.

4. "GM's Bet to Take on Tesla (TSLA): An Electric Hummer," Bloomberg, December 17, 2020, https://www.bloomberg.com/news

/articles/2020-12-17/gm-s-bet-to-take-on-tesla-tsla-an
-electric-hummer.

5. David Welch, "GM Deepens EV Bet with 35% Budget Boost
and 30 New Models," Bloomberg, Novmber 19, 2020, https://
www.bloomberg.com/news/articles/2020-11-19/gm-ups
-ev-budget-by-one-third-plans-30-battery-powered-models.

6. Jeanne Whalen, "U.S. Restricts Tech Exports to China's Biggest Semiconductor Manufacturer in Escalation of Trade Ten-
sions," *Washington Post*, September 26, 2020, https://www
.washingtonpost.com/technology/2020/09/26/us-restricts
-exports-chinas-smic/.

7. Arjun Kharpal, "China's Most Important Chipmaker SMIC
Could Be a Big Winner from the Global Semiconductor Shortage," CNBC, March 1, 2021, https://www.cnbc.com/2021
/03/02/china-semiconductor-maker-smic-could-be-a-winner
-from-global-chip-shortage.html.

8. "Automotive Chips to Be Hurt by Renesas Fire, CEO Says,"
Bloomberg, March 21, 2021, https://www.bloomberg.com/news
/articles/2021-03-21/automotive-chip-supplies-to-be-hurt
-by-renesas-fire-ceo-says.

9. Neal E. Boudette and Coral Davenport, "G.M. Will Sell Only
Zero-Emission Vehicles by 2035," *The New York Times*, January
28, 2021, https://www.nytimes.com/2021/01/28/business/gm
-zero-emission-vehicles.html.

EPILOGUE

1. "GM Tells Bolt Owners to Park 50 Feet Away from Other Cars,"
Bloomberg, September 15, 2021, https://www.bloomberg.com
/news/articles/2021-09-15/gm-tells-some-bolt-owners-to
-park-50-feet-away-from-other-cars.

2. "GM's Barra Dismissed Cruise CEO Ammann Over Mission,
IPO," Bloomberg, December 19, 2021, https://www.bloomberg
.com/news/articles/2021-12-19/gm-s-barra-dismissed-cruise
-ceo-ammann-over-mission-ipo-timing.

3. "GM Bids a Brusque Farewell to the CEO of Cruise," Bloomberg, December 17, 2021, https://www.bloomberg.com/news

/articles/2021-12-17/gm-bids-a-brusque-farewell-to-the-ceo -of-cruise.

4. "Hot, New Electric Cars That Are Coming Soon," Consumer Reports, March 3, 2022, https://www.consumerreports.org /hybrids-evs/hot-new-electric-cars-are-coming-soon -a1000197429/.

5. Jameson Dow, "Cadillac Lyriq Sells Out in 19 Minutes—Auto-makers Still Underestimate EV Demand," Electrek, September 18, 2021, https://electrek.co/2021/09/18/cadillac-lyriq-sells-out -in-19-minutes-automakers-still-underestimating-ev-demand/.

6. Joseph White, "GM Plans Six-Fold Increase in 2022 Electric Truck, SUV Production —Sources," Reuters, February 8, 2022, https://www.reuters.com/article/gm-electric-production -idCNL1N2UJ1IY.

INDEX

Rivian Automotive, 195–198, 215
Rivian R1T, 196, 198
Robinson, Mike, 79
robots, 19, 173
Rodriguez, Julio, 168
Rometti, Ginny, 143, 146
Russia, 36, 92
Russo, Patricia, 64
Ryan, Tim, 124

Saab, 39
SAIC, 93
Salesky, Bryan, 176
Sandefur, Scott, 116, 134
Sanders, Bernie, 122, 125
Saturday Night Live, 4, 74
Saturn, 20, 39
Saturn Ion, 75
Saturn L-series, 31–32
Scaringe, R.J., 195–196
Schwarzman, Stephen, 148
self-driving vehicles
    Cruise, 183–192, 202, 212, 220–222
    DARPA Challenge, 174–176
    deaths, 190–191
    disengagements issue, 188
    early history of, 176
    fundraising and investors, 179,
        187–188
    Google and Waymo, 9, 90, 176–180,
        186–192, 211, 215–216
    hiring binge for tech talent, 206
    layoffs (2018) and, 127
    lidar technology, 176
    Origin shuttle, 191–192, 212
    Super Cruise, 181–182, 202, 211, 221
    taxis, self-driving, 129
    ten-year growth plan and, 202
    Tesla Autopilot system, 177–180,
        187
    Ultra Cruise, 211, 221
semiconductor supply crisis, 200–201,
    207–208
share buybacks, 90, 122
Silicon Valley, 88
Simcoe, Mike, 98, 104
Sloan, Alfred, 7, 11–12, 19, 50, 87,
    205, 208
Smale, John, 21
Smith, Jack, 21, 23, 98–99
Smith, John, 38–39
Smith, Roger, 19–20, 23–24, 28
SoftBank Vision Fund, 187

software capabilities, 210–211
Solso, Tim, 7–8, 64–65, 81
South Africa, 97
South America, 91, 180–181
Southeast Asia, 87, 91–92
"Speak Up for Safety" program, 81
Special Purpose Acquisition
    Companies (SPACs), 167
Stempel, Robert, 21–22
Stephens, Tom, 51–52, 58
Stephenson, Carol, 64
Stevens, Chuck, 87, 95
Stewart, Gordon, 33
strikes
    Flint, 25–27
    Lordstown, 132–134, 152–153,
        158–159, 162
    Oshawa, 119–120
styling, automotive, 12
Super Cruise, 181–182, 202, 211

tariffs, 142, 143, 149–150
Tavares, Carlos, 93, 95–96, 222
Tavel, Josh, 113, 193–199
team leaders, 28
Tesla
    Autopilot hands-free driving
        system, 177–180, 187
    electric cars, 6, 56
    luxury car market and, 6, 105
    market value, 89, 200
    sales and losses, 106, 107
    as threat, 89, 105
    upgrades, 216
Tesla Cybertruck, 198
Tesla Model 3, 59, 89, 103, 193–194
Tesla Model S, 9, 59, 60, 89
Tesla Model X, 89
Tesla Model Y, 210, 219
Thailand, 87
363 sale, 40
Thrun, Sebastian, 175
tool and die workers, 14
Torfeh, Mo, 15–16
Toyota, 16–17, 84–85, 87, 177
Toyota Corolla, 31, 157
Toyota Highlander, 212
Toyota Prius, 33, 54, 78, 108
Trans-Pacific Partnership, 137
Treasury Department Auto Task Force,
    39–40
T. Rowe Price Associates, 188
Trudeau, Justin, 119, 124

ABOUT THE AUTHOR

DAVID WELCH is the Detroit bureau chief for Bloomberg News and also writes about the auto industry for *Bloomberg Business-week* magazine. He has been with Bloomberg for twelve years and was the Detroit bureau chief for *BusinessWeek* before that. He has written a dozen cover stories for *Bloomberg Business-week* and six about GM, including a September 2019 cover profile of Mary Barra. He has also written many articles and news-breaking coverage about all the major auto companies and related topics. Welch's work has won him awards from organizations such as the Society of American Business Editors and Writers, Business Journalist of the Year Awards, the Clarion Awards, the New York Press Club, the Deadline Club, and the Society of Professional Journalists.

DISCARDED
WORTHINGTON LIBRARIES